The Legal Memo: 50 Exercises for Mastery

The Legal Memo:
50 Exercises for Mastery

Practice for the New Legal Writer

Cassandra L. Hill
DEAN AND PROFESSOR OF LAW
NORTHERN ILLINOIS UNIVERSITY
COLLEGE OF LAW

D'Andra Millsap Shu
CO-DIRECTOR OF LAWYERING PROCESS AND
VISITING INSTRUCTOR OF LAW
TEXAS SOUTHERN UNIVERSITY
THURGOOD MARSHALL SCHOOL OF LAW

Katherine T. Vukadin
PROFESSOR OF LAW
SOUTH TEXAS COLLEGE OF LAW HOUSTON

CAROLINA ACADEMIC PRESS
Durham, North Carolina

ISBN: 978-1-5310-1683-8
e-ISBN: 978-1-5310-1684-5
LCCN: 2020943581

Carolina Academic Press
700 Kent Street
Durham, NC 27701
Telephone (919) 489-7486
Fax (919) 493-5668
www.caplaw.com

Printed in the United States of America

Each year, we are honored to teach students who come from all backgrounds, who yearn to be attorneys, and who put in the work despite every obstacle. We dedicate this book to you.

Cassandra L. Hill is the dean and a professor of law at the Northern Illinois University College of Law. She was previously the associate dean for academic affairs at the Thurgood Marshall School of Law at Texas Southern University and served on a three-member leadership team with the law school's acting dean. She also served as associate dean for research and faculty development and director of legal writing.

Dean Hill received her J.D. from Howard University School of Law, where she graduated as valedictorian. She then clerked for the Honorable Vanessa D. Gilmore, United States District Court for the Southern District of Texas. She practiced with the law firm of Baker Botts L.L.P. in the tax/employee benefits section. Dean Hill then began her teaching career at UCLA School of Law. Her scholarship focuses on pedagogy, learning theory, and assessment in legal education. She has presented and written extensively in these areas. She is the co-author of *Legal Analysis: 100 Exercises for Mastery* (with Professor Katherine Vukadin), which is now in its second edition and has been adopted at more than twenty-five law schools nationwide. She is chair of the American Bar Association (ABA) Section of Legal Education and Admissions to the Bar Conferences and Programming Committee and has experience as a site-team evaluator with the ABA. Dean Hill was the first elected African American member of the Board of Directors for the Legal Writing Institute (LWI), and she was a managing editor of the LWI Monograph Series.

D'Andra Millsap Shu is co-director of the legal writing program and a visiting instructor of law at the Thurgood Marshall School of Law at Texas Southern University. She teaches legal writing and appellate litigation. She received her J.D. from the University of Houston Law Center, where she was class valedictorian and editor in chief of the *Houston Law Review.*

Before teaching, Professor Shu spent about half of her twenty-plus years of practice working at two large national law firms, Baker Botts L.L.P. and Morgan, Lewis & Bockius. For the other half, she worked at three appellate courts—the Fifth Circuit Court of Appeals, the Texas Supreme Court, and Texas's Fourteenth Court of Appeals. She brings this wealth of practical experience to her teaching, guiding students to connect the importance of their classroom learning with the demands of law practice. She knows first hand what judges, partners, and clients value in legal writing, and she helps her students perfect the skills necessary to write to these standards.

Professor Shu's research interests include legal education, legal writing pedagogy, disability law, and food allergy law. She has co-authored short pieces on legal writing and written two full-length law review articles on food allergy bullying, which appear in the *Marquette Law Review* and the *University of Colorado Law Review*.

Katherine T. Vukadin is a professor of law at the South Texas College of Law Houston, where she teaches legal research and writing. She received her J.D. from the University of Texas School of Law and began her legal career as an associate in the trial department at Baker Botts L.L.P.

Professor Vukadin first taught legal writing at the University of Houston Law Center, then at the Thurgood Marshall School of Law at Texas Southern University, and now at the South Texas College of Law Houston. Her research and teaching interests include legal education, legal writing pedagogy, ERISA, and healthcare policy and regulation.

She is the co-author (with Dean Cassandra Hill) of *Legal Analysis: 100 Exercises for Mastery*, now in its second edition. Her articles have appeared in publications including *The Second Draft*; the *Richmond Law Review*; the *Yale Journal of Health Policy, Law, and Ethics*; the *Buffalo Law Review*; and the *Tulsa Law Review*. She presents regularly at regional and national legal writing conferences.

Professor Vukadin specializes in using innovative teaching techniques to make legal writing compelling and accessible to all students. She has taught legal writing to foreign law students seeking an American LL.M. degree and designed a class for law students needing further writing practice. Professor Vukadin has learned that with commitment, practice, and patience, students can master the essentials of legal writing.

Acknowledgments

We appreciate and thank our national and institutional colleagues, the broader legal writing community, our students, and our families.

We thank our law student Content Consultants: Gisela A. Aguilar, Graciela E. Garcia, Charles Graham, Jr., Joitza Henriquez, Amanda G. Hoover, Abreante' A. Jones, Caroline E. Lovallo, Valerie Medina, Adaiwu Nwaiwu, Cindy G. Perez, and Terralyn Wilburn. The Content Consultants worked the problems, gave us their frank and valuable critique, and advised us how to make the book more useful. Our Principal Content Consultant, Alexandria Law Monroe, committed to our project early and stayed with us to the end. We appreciate her excellent critiques, flexibility, and professionalism. Professor Shelley Ward Bennett also provided valuable critique, suggestions, and encouragement.

Cassandra Hill thanks her husband, William Grogan, for his support, inspiration, patience, and humor along the way. She thanks her mother, Etta M. Hill, for her support, prayers, and wisdom. She also thanks her family and friends who have supported her throughout her career. She thanks her many brilliant students, whose dedication and success inspire her every day.

D'Andra Millsap Shu thanks her students for inspiring this work. Her desire to meet student requests for additional skills practice helped generate the idea for this book. Her colleagues in the Thurgood Marshall administration and faculty have been very supportive of this first book endeavor. She thanks her husband, Glen, and her sons, Nathan and Ryan, for their patience and encouragement throughout this process.

Katherine Vukadin thanks her supportive colleagues and administration at the South Texas College of Law Houston. She thanks her husband, Davor Vukadin, for his encouragement and constant support, and her mom, Anne Traverse, for her love and her faith in this project. She thanks her children, Chris, Sophie, and Nick, for their love and patience. She thanks her students for their commitment to the law and for the creativity and joy they bring to the classroom.

Contents

Expanded Table of Contents

Master Skills Tested Chart

CHAPTER	SKILL	SUBSKILL (IF ANY)	EXERCISE TESTED
2: HEADING AND INTRODUCTION	Content	client information date specific issue	1, 2 1, 2 1, 2
	Format	alignment keep it short	1, 2 1, 2
3: QUESTION PRESENTED AND BRIEF ANSWER	Consistency	language same format same order number of questions and answers	5, 8 8 8 8
	Stands Alone		3, 4, 5, 7, 8
	Accepted Format	under/does/when whether multi-sentence	3, 4, 5, 6, 7, 8 3, 4, 5, 7 3, 4, 5, 7, 8
	Legal Context		4, 5, 6, 7, 8
	Precise Question		4, 5, 6, 7, 8
	Facts	specific determinative objective	3, 4, 5, 6, 7, 8 3, 4, 5, 6, 7, 8 4, 6, 7
	Conclusion Not Assumed		5

CHAPTER	SKILL	SUBSKILL (IF ANY)	EXERCISE TESTED
3: QUESTION PRESENTED AND BRIEF ANSWER (*continued*)	Readability	subject/verb placement	5, 7, 8
		punctuation	5, 6, 7, 8
		conciseness	6, 7, 8
	Answer	short answer first	3, 4, 5, 6, 7, 8
		echo question language	3, 4, 5, 6, 7, 8
	Conclusion-Rule-Application-Conclusion Format		3, 4, 5, 6, 7, 8
4: STATEMENT OF FACTS	Fact Selection	relevant details	9, 10, 13, 14, 15, 16
		negative facts	13, 15
		conflicting evidence	15
		specificity	13, 14, 15, 16
		dates and time indicators	12
	Structure	logical order	11, 12, 15, 16
		paragraphing	11, 15, 16
		topic sentences	11, 16
		bridging words	11, 16
		good flow	12, 15, 16
	Tone and Language	objective	9, 10
		not dramatic	10, 14, 16
		no stereotypes	10
	Facts Only	no opinions	10, 14
		no legal conclusions	14
	Party Descriptions		14

CHAPTER	SKILL	SUBSKILL (IF ANY)	EXERCISE TESTED
5: DISCUSSION			
A: ROADMAP	Conclusion	comprehensive	17, 18
		reasoning explained	17, 18
	Legal Background	overall rule	17, 18
		legal context	17, 18
	Memo Contents	excluded items	18
		included items	17, 18
		relationship between items	17, 18
	Nuts and Bolts	no issue-specific material	17, 18
		order follows memo structure	17, 18
B: DISCUSSION CONCLUSIONS	Answer the Question		19, 20
	Give a Reason When Possible		19, 20
	Keep It Short		20
	Consistency	vary wording but not substance	19, 20
		consistent prediction language	19, 20
C: RULE AND EXPLANATION	Rule Contours	choice of authority	22, 28
		broad to narrow	21, 24, 25, 28, 29, 32
		rule tailoring	22, 24, 25, 27, 28, 29, 30, 32
	Treatment Depth	parenthetical	26, 29, 30
		short explanation	26, 29, 30
		case illustration	29, 30

CHAPTER	SKILL	SUBSKILL (IF ANY)	EXERCISE TESTED
C: RULE AND EXPLANATION (*continued*)	Case Illustration	introductory sentence	23, 24, 27, 30, 31, 32
		fact selection	23, 24, 27, 30, 31, 32
		reasoning and holding	23, 24, 27, 30, 31
	Multiple Case Illustrations		31
	Nuts and Bolts	citations	21, 23, 24, 25, 30, 31, 32
		no client facts	27, 32
		quotations	24, 25, 30, 32
		past tense	24, 27, 30, 31, 32
D: APPLICATION	Structure	thesis statement	36, 37, 43, 44
		arguments rather than cases	36, 43, 44
		base arguments on rules	39, 40, 42, 43, 44
		analysis parallels case illustration	37, 38, 43, 44
	Effective Analogies	how to analogize	33, 34, 43, 44
		relevant comparisons	33, 34, 35, 41, 43, 44
		proximity or pattern	35, 38, 41
	Show Your Work	be specific	35, 39, 40, 43, 44
		weave client facts and case information	37, 38, 41, 42, 43, 44
		tie back to the rule	37, 39, 40, 44
	Nuts and Bolts	citation	38, 39, 42, 43, 44
		objective tone	35, 40, 43

CHAPTER	SKILL	SUBSKILL (IF ANY)	EXERCISE TESTED
E: COUNTER-ARGUMENT AND REBUTTAL	Structure	detail the counterarguments	46, 47, 48
		separate multiple counterarguments	47
		explicitly rebut	46, 47, 48
	Substance	only viable counterarguments	45, 47
		no new law	45
		rebut with new analysis	46, 47, 48
	Clear Transitions		46, 47, 48
6: MEMO CONCLUSION	Keep It Short		49, 50
	Give the Reasons		49, 50
	Consistency		49, 50
	Give Any Advice		49, 50
	Nuts and Bolts	answer immediately	49, 50
		no citations	50
7: EMAIL MEMOS	Format	short sentences and paragraphs	51, 52, 53, 54
		headings and labels	52, 54
		white space	51, 52, 54
	Language	less formal	53, 54
		professional	51, 53, 54
		grammatical	51, 54
	Content	specific subject line	51, 53, 54
		concise	51, 53, 54
		efficient	51, 53, 54
		rule-based analysis	53, 54
		few cites	53, 54

The Legal Memo: 50 Exercises for Mastery

Chapter 1

How to Use This Book

The legal memo is the writer's expression of legal analysis, providing a complete, reasoned answer to a specific question. To succeed as a first-year law student, a summer associate, or a new lawyer, a legal writer must be able to produce a proficient memo. To do this, the writer must first master a series of distinct and crucial skills: fact selection, narrowing of the specific legal issue, correct rule formulation, and accurate application of the law to the client's facts, to name but a few. To gain a solid footing in this new area, emerging legal writers need timely and efficient practice to perfect the skills they have learned in class. Legal writers will find the practice they need in this book.

The law student first encounters the memo in the 1L year. Bombarded with novel information, the first-year law student may hesitate when piecing together a first memo. The emerging legal writer may broach high-stakes memo assignments or summer associate projects with trepidation, straining to apply the precise steps and conventions set out in first-year lectures and textbooks. Using this book, legal writers can build on their existing foundation and practice what they have learned from professors and primary coursebooks.

Particular Audiences. Legal writing professors, academic support professionals, law students, and all emerging legal writers can benefit from this book. For legal writing professors, the book provides more than fifty opportunities for students to reinforce memo skills learned in class. Instead of spending time crafting new material, professors can assign these exercises; students can self-check at the back of the book for half of the answers, and professors can grade answers using the teacher's manual for the other half. Academic support professionals too can assign exercises to assist students needing extra help with the memo's nuances. The book need not be used in conjunction with a class; independent legal writers can check their work using the even-numbered exercises at the back of the book. Any legal writer using these exercises will develop a keen understanding of the memo's various components and necessary skills.

Content and Sections. Each chapter targets a particular memo section, beginning with the heading and introduction. The book next addresses the question presented and brief answer, and then the statement of facts. Next come the roadmap, initial and final conclusions, rule and explanation, and analysis, ending with the counter-argument and rebuttal. Additional material includes bonus exercises on email memos as well as two full sample memos, one addressing a single issue and another addressing two. Both memos contain annotations highlighting the various memo skills demonstrated.

Some employers or instructors may vary in the sections that their memos include. The introduction, for example, may or may not appear in a memo, depending on the assigning person's preference. The legal writer should defer to the assigner's particular norms.

Introduction and Skills. Each chapter begins with an introduction that lists and describes the skills to be covered and identifies which exercises cover each skill. Those skills are also set out in a detailed table of contents at the front of this book and in a freestanding chart, located immediately after the detailed table of contents, that cross-references which exercises test those skills. The writer can thus work through all the exercises for complete coverage of that memo section or can select fewer exercises to target certain skills. While some exercises might echo the facts, concept, or legal rule from another exercise, each exercise stands alone. They can be completed in any order, with no need to learn an overarching set of facts or legal principles.

Time. Each exercise is designed to take approximately fifteen or thirty minutes. Exercise 54 concerning email memos takes about sixty minutes, so students have time to recast a full memo as a concise email memo.

Fifteen-minute exercises ("Lightning Round") allow professors to teach specific skills and then immediately reinforce them within the same class period; independent legal writers too may want quick practice.

For more in-depth practice, the book contains exercises taking about thirty minutes ("Deeper Dive"). The thirty-minute exercises go deeper into the material while bringing together several of the skills.

Students and professors will have very little ramp-up time and can get right into the skills practice because each exercise is independent, not depending on a master set of facts or the answers to a prior problem.

Paradigm for a Unit of Legal Analysis. This book uses the CREAC paradigm: Conclusion, Rule, Explanation, Analysis (or Application), and Conclusion. Where no explanation of the rule is required, the paradigm is CRAC: Conclusion, Rule, Analysis (or Application), and Conclusion. Although the substance of a legal argument varies little from one law school to another, the paradigm may be called something different. Some law schools use "TREAT," meaning Thesis, Rule, Explanation, Application, Thesis; others use "CRRPAC," meaning Conclusion, Rule, Rule Proof, Application, and Conclusion. Regardless of the name, the core content generally does not vary.

Adapted Law. The law included in the book is often altered, supplemented, or invented for pedagogical reasons. The law included here may differ from the law of any particular jurisdiction. Readers should therefore rely on other sources when seeking black-letter law.

Answers. Each exercise has a corresponding answer, explained in detail. The answers to the even-numbered exercises appear at the back of this main volume. Students can use these answers to work independently and check their own progress. The remaining answers are provided in a teacher's manual, so professors can assign exercises and check students' memo skills.

Let Us Know. With guided practice, the aspiring legal writer can become proficient in the essential skill of writing a legal memo. This book provides practice for each part of the memo, so the new legal writer can broach every memo assignment with confidence. If the book helps you, please share your success with us. If we can make the book more useful, we would like to know that too. Please stay in touch with us at 50ExercisesForMastery@gmail.com.

Chapter 2

Heading and Introduction

Summary of Skills Tested

The heading and introduction set out the memo's context and subject. They ensure that the correct reader receives the memo and that it can be properly filed.

Heading: Content and Format. The memo's heading provides important practical information, such as the recipient, author, date, and subject. Ensure that the date included is the date the memo was actually transmitted. The date should be in expanded format, with the month spelled out and all four digits of the year included. The subject or "re" line should state the memo's specific issue—this ensures that if the case requires multiple memos, a busy lawyer can quickly find the appropriate one. This can also help future colleagues who might search the firm's memo bank for similar research. The heading should follow office conventions regarding the file number. Keep the entries aligned and provide white space between the lines so the heading is visually appealing and easy to read.

SKILLS TESTED IN THIS CHAPTER	
SKILL	EXERCISE
Content	1, 2
Format	1, 2

Introduction: Content and Format. While a memo almost invariably contains a heading, some do not include an introduction. Follow your assigning person's lead as to whether one should be included. If included, the introduction should be short and capture the memo's substance: the parties, the client, the issue, a brief factual background, and the outcome.

The introduction should not contain detailed or extensive facts—those belong in the statement of facts. The introduction gives only a high-level summary of the context rather than specific facts or the complete story of the case.

The following exercises will show you how to draft effective headings and introductions. You can find annotated sample answers to the even-numbered exercises at the back of this book. For examples of headings and introductions, refer to the sample memos in Chapter 8.

Exercise 1

 *Lightning Round*

Skills Tested (explained on pages 7–8):

1. Content (client information, date, specific issue)
2. Format (alignment, keep it short)

Examples: The sample memos in Chapter 8 contain examples of headings and introductions (see pages 145, 151).

Factual Background: You are assigned to prosecute Frank Smith, who robbed a convenience store while pointing to his Swiss Army knife. The knife was unopened and remained in Smith's front pants pocket during the robbery, but the knife was partially visible. Smith demanded money as the clerk opened the register to give Smith his change. The clerk complied out of fear of the knife.

Legal Principles: If the knife is considered a "deadly weapon," then Smith could receive additional penalties for the crime. To be a "deadly weapon," a weapon need not actually be used; it is sufficient that the weapon is displayed in a manner conveying an express or implied threat that serious bodily injury or death will be inflicted if the aggressor's desire is not satisfied. *Lucero v. State*, 915 S.W.2d 612, 612 (Tenn. 2010).

Exercise: You are analyzing whether the Swiss Army knife can be deemed a deadly weapon when used as Smith did during the robbery.

(1) Laura Wu, the senior prosecutor, will be trying the robbery case against Frank Smith, and she has asked you for a memo on the deadly weapon issue. The case is file number 20/544:FS. In this prosecutor's office, the convention is to place the file number in parentheses at the start of the re line. Draft a suitable heading for a memo on this issue.

(2) Draft an introduction for the memo. Be sure to identify the parties and the issue.

Exercise 2

 *Lightning Round*

....

Skills Tested (explained on pages 7–8):

1. Content (client information, date, specific issue)
2. Format (alignment, keep it short)

....

Examples: The sample memos in Chapter 8 contain examples of headings and introductions (see pages 145, 151).

Exercise: Below are sample headings and introduction paragraphs for a memo regarding a slip and fall negligence claim against your client, Big K Groceries. Which one of each is most effective and why?

Headings:

(1)   TO: Lee Freedman
FROM: Valena Litman
REGARDING: Negligence

(2)   TO: Lee Freedman

FROM: Valena Litman

DATE: September 2, 2020

RE: 006945.004, Big K Groceries, Proximate Cause and Damages
for Slip and Fall Negligence Claim

(3)   FROM: Valena Litman

TO: Lee Freedman

DATE: 9/2/20

RE: 006945.004, Big K's Negligence Claim

Introductions:

(1)   Leah Beety sued our client, Big K Groceries, for negligence after she slipped and fell in a puddle of spilled coffee in one of Big K's stores. This claim will likely fail for two reasons. First, Big K likely did not breach any duty because it had recently cleaned the floor. Second, an earlier car accident, not the fall, likely caused Beety's damages.

(2)   Beety's negligence claim against Big K Groceries will fail. The elements of negligence are duty, breach of duty, causation, and damages. Liability flows from conduct that causes reasonably foreseeable harm. A harm is foreseeable if a person of ordinary intelligence should have reasonably anticipated the danger. Beety slipped in a puddle of coffee that, according to video footage, had been on the floor for under one minute. Big K had cleaned the floor five minutes earlier. It is not foreseeable that failing to monitor the floor for one minute would cause someone to fall. Moreover, Beety's damages are based on a back injury, but a car accident two months before the fall caused her back problems, not the fall.

Chapter 3

Question Presented and Brief Answer

Summary of Skills Tested

The question presented sets out the memo's legal context, the precise issue at hand, and the specific facts that will determine the question's answer; the brief answer is a high-level overview of the answer to the question presented. Both serve the crucial function of encapsulating a larger part of the memo. In a busy law office, the assigning partner may read the question presented and brief answer and go no further. Thus, although they are short sections of the memo, the question presented and brief answer play an important role and should be crafted with care and attention to detail. To write an effective question presented and brief answer, practice and apply the skills and features set out below.

SKILLS TESTED IN THIS CHAPTER	
SKILL	EXERCISE
Consistency	5, 8
Stands Alone	3, 4, 5, 7, 8
Accepted Format	3, 4, 5, 6, 7, 8
Legal Context	4, 5, 6, 7, 8
Precise Question	4, 5, 6, 7, 8
Facts	3, 4, 5, 6, 7, 8
Conclusion Not Assumed	5
Readability	5, 6, 7, 8
Answer	3, 4, 5, 6, 7, 8
Conclusion-Rule-Application-Conclusion Format	3, 4, 5, 6, 7, 8

Consistency. The question presented and brief answer function as a unit and thus should be parallel and consistent. Each question presented should have a corresponding brief answer, and if the memo contains multiple issues, the questions presented and brief answers on each issue should appear in the same order. A question presented may refer to the parties by either their proper names or their category, such as "the Bank of Smithville" or "a bank." Whichever the writer chooses, however, the question presented must be consistent, both internally and with the brief answer. Ensure that the answer's language echoes key language from the question presented.

Stands Alone. The question presented and its answer together should be self-contained, covering all the reader needs to grasp what is at stake in the memo.

A. The Question Presented

The following skills are particularly useful in drafting a question presented.

Accepted Format. The writer can choose from three principal formats for a question presented: whether, under/does/when, or multi-sentence. The choice will depend on the assigning person's preference, the writer's preference, and the suitability of each format to the particular issue. Any of the three formats is an acceptable choice, but the whether format should be used with caution to avoid producing an unnecessarily unwieldy question presented. Also, a question in the whether format should end with a period, not a question mark (because it is not a grammatical question). In a multi-issue memo, each question presented should be in the same format.

Legal Context. The question tells the reader what law will apply—perhaps a specific statute, a jurisdiction's law, or an area of the law.

Precise Question. The question presented should showcase the precise issue. Be careful to raise exactly the question that the assigning person has described. For example, if the assignment is to address whether a duty exists, the memo should not ask whether a party was negligent or liable—both of those issues would be outside the assignment's scope. If the writer does want to comment on the question's effect on another issue, that comment should be placed in the memo's conclusion.

Facts. The facts within the question presented should be specific and objective. The writer maintains objectivity by choosing not only facts that support the writer's conclusion (or affirmative argument) but also facts that support the counterargument. If the facts selected all support one side, the reader may not see why a full analysis is needed.

Conclusion Not Assumed. The question presented should keep the question open. Accordingly, avoid using language that dictates a certain outcome. If the question, for example, is whether a person was negligent, the facts should not state that the person did not exercise ordinary care, as that could indicate that the person was, by definition, negligent. Instead, the writer should state the facts that suggest that answer as well as one or two that suggest the opposing answer, if any exist.

Readability. The question presented includes several components and delivers a large amount of information. Even as the question contains all its appropriate parts, it must remain readable to be effective. To ensure the question's readability, the writer should be concise, keep the subject and verb as close together as possible, and use punctuation with care.

B. The Brief Answer

As with the question presented, an effective brief answer calls for particular skills.

Answer. The brief answer should first give a short prediction of how the question turns out. The reader should know your answer immediately. Be careful to answer the question asked, and use clear prediction language such as "Probably yes" or "Almost certainly not."

Conclusion-Rule-Application-Conclusion Format. The conclusion is paramount and should come first in the brief answer. After the conclusion, add a concise version of the most crucial and outcome-determinative rules. While most writers do not cite authority after the brief answer's rule of law, some do. So, observe the assigning person's preference in this regard. The most troublesome aspect of the brief answer tends to be the application. Analogical reasoning is of course not possible at this point because no case facts have yet appeared in the memo; the writer can still state specific client facts and describe how they meet or do not meet the rule. A reader wanting to know more will proceed to the full analysis. Last, a conclusion wraps up the brief answer and lets the reader know that the section has ended.

Practice crafting expert questions presented and brief answers by using the exercises that follow. You can check your work against the even-numbered annotated sample answers in the back of this book. The sample memos in Chapter 8 show examples of questions presented and brief answers for three issues.

Exercise 3

Part A: Question Presented

 *Lightning Round*

Skills Tested (explained on page 14):

1. Stands Alone
2. Accepted Format (under/does/when, whether, multi-sentence)
3. Facts (specific, determinative)

Examples: The sample memos in Chapter 8 contain examples of questions presented and brief answers (see pages 145–46, 151–52).

Legal Background: One element of an adverse possession claim is the title owner's notice of the adverse use. Unless notice is actual, the use must be open and notorious so that the title-holder's notice may be presumed. *Tex-Wis Co. v. Johnson*, 534 S.W.2d 895, 901 (Tex. 1976). To be open and notorious, the use must be visible and obvious to an ordinary title owner. *Zimmerman v. Chicago Title Ins. Co.*, 28 S.W.3d 584, 586 (Tex. App. 1999).

Factual Background: You represent Marsha Herrera, who has title to ten acres of land in the Texas Hill Country. She visits the property about once per month to check on the property and perform any maintenance. One day, Herrera was surprised by a letter from GasNow, a local natural gas company, asserting the right to keep its large gas pipes permanently under her property. Herrera had no idea that any pipes ran under the property, and that right appears nowhere in the property records. GasNow bases its claim on the following facts: (1) the gas lines have existed under the property for the statutory adverse possession period; (2) the gas lines are three feet wide; and (3) when GasNow placed the pipes, it also placed shiny metal plates, about the size of a dinner plate, thirty feet apart, flush with the ground, along the pipes' route.

Legal Issue: Do GasNow's actions on the Herrera property satisfy the open and notorious element of an adverse possession claim?

Exercise: Two different versions of a question presented are set out below. Each one is missing facts from the problem. Please add the facts to the question, and then determine which format (under/does/when or whether) is more effective for this problem.

Questions Presented:

(1) Under Texas law, does GasNow's use of the Herrera property satisfy the open and notorious element of adverse possession, when _____ _____?

(2) Whether GasNow can establish the open and notorious element of adverse possession under Texas law, when GasNow _____ _____.

Part B: Brief Answer

 Lightning Round

....

Skills Tested (explained on page 15):

1. Answer (short answer first, echo question language)
2. Conclusion-Rule-Application-Conclusion Format

....

Legal Background: Same as above.

Factual Background: Same as above.

Legal Issue: Same as above.

Exercise: A brief answer for the issue in Part A above is set out below. The parts, however, are out of order. In addition, there is an extra section. Please put the parts in order and state which section is not needed. Please explain your reasoning.

A.   To establish the open and notorious element of adverse possession, a claimant's use must be plainly visible, creating a presumption of notice to the title owner.

B.   Probably not.

C.   Thus, GasNow's use of the Herrera property probably does not satisfy the open and notorious element of adverse possession because an ordinary owner would not easily see GasNow's use.

D.   GasNow's gas pipes were not visible to the naked eye because they were underground. Although GasNow also installed metal plates at thirty-foot intervals along the pipes' route, those too were not easily visible, unless the owner stood very close to or above them.

continued

E.   A use was open and notorious when a utility company placed utility poles at twenty-five foot intervals across a rural piece of property. *Adams v. Gomez*, 33 S.W.2d 45, 47 (Tex. 1988). Although the land was in a remote area that a typical owner might not visit frequently, the use was still sufficient to give notice. *Id.*

Exercise 4

Part A: Question Presented

 *Lightning Round*

Skills Tested (explained on page 14):

1. Stands Alone
2. Accepted Format (under/does/when, whether, multi-sentence)
3. Legal Context
4. Precise Question
5. Facts (specific, determinative, objective)

Examples: The sample memos in Chapter 8 contain examples of questions presented and brief answers (see pages 145–46, 151–52).

Legal Background: For a parent's rights to be terminated, the State must establish (1) one condition from a list of statutory conditions and (2) that termination is in the child's best interest. Tex. Fam. Code Ann. § 161.001. Courts determine the child's best interest using factors such as the child's desires, the child's present and future physical and emotional needs, the present and future emotional and physical danger to the child, available programs to promote the child's best interest, the stability of the current or proposed home, a parent's acts or omissions, and any excuse for the acts or omissions. *Id.*

Factual Background: Because she needed to care for her ill mother, Sara Ramada left her child, four-year-old J.M., in the care of her boyfriend, who Ramada later learned used drugs around the child. Protective Services intervened and took the child into foster care. Its inspection showed Ramada's apartment was messy and dirty, but after her mother recovered, Ramada kept her apartment clean and stocked with appropriate food. Protective Services asked Ramada not to see her boyfriend anymore, as he used drugs; nevertheless, Ramada continued to see him. Ramada completed two online parenting courses with scores of 95%. Ramada and J.M. have an affectionate relationship, and J.M. is always delighted to see her mother.

Legal Issue: Would termination of Sara Ramada's parental rights be in the child's best interest?

Exercise: The following are three different versions of a question presented for a memorandum on this issue. Which one is most effective? If a question is not effective, why not? Please make at least three specific observations about each of the questions below.

(1) A parent's rights can be terminated if, among other things, termination would be in the child's best interest. Sara Ramada shares an affectionate relationship with her child, earned high scores in her parenting classes, and remedied the messy state of her apartment. Can Sara Ramada's parental rights to J.M. be terminated?

(2) Whether termination is in the best interest of J.M., when J.M. has an affectionate relationship with her mother.

(3) Under Texas law, would termination of Ramada's parental rights be in J.M.'s best interest, when Ramada shares an affectionate relationship with J.M., earned high scores in her parenting classes, and remedied the messy state of her apartment, but persisted in seeing a known drug user?

Part B: Brief Answer

 Lightning Round

....

Skills Tested (explained on page 15):

1. Answer (short answer first, echo question language)
2. Conclusion-Rule-Application-Conclusion Format

....

Legal Background: Same as above.

Factual Background: Same as above.

Legal Issue: Same as above.

Exercise: The following are three different versions of a brief answer to the question presented in Part A above. Which one is most effective? If an answer is not effective, why not? Please make at least three specific observations about each of the brief answers below.

(1)   Probably not. Before a parent's rights can be terminated, termination must be in the child's best interest. Courts determine the child's best interest using factors such as the child's desires, the child's needs, potential danger to the child, available helpful programs, housing stability, a parent's acts and omissions, and potential excuses for those acts and omissions. Thus, the court should not terminate Ramada's rights.

(2)   Ramada was generally a good parent, and her child liked to see her. To terminate a parent's rights, termination must be in the child's best interest. Thus, the court should not terminate Ramada's rights.

(3)   Probably not. To terminate a parent's rights, termination must be in the child's best interest. Courts determine the child's best interest using various factors, including the child's desires, the child's needs, potential danger to the child, available helpful programs, housing stability, a parent's acts and omissions, and potential excuses for those acts and omissions. Ramada kept her child safe, maintained appropriate housing, and has a positive relationship with her child. Due to her own mother's illness, Ramada left her child with someone who used drugs; Ramada continues to see this person. On balance, however, terminating Ramada's rights would not be in her child's best interest.

Exercise 5

Part A: Question Presented

 Lightning Round

Skills Tested (explained on pages 13–15):

1. Consistency (language)
2. Stands Alone
3. Accepted Format (under/does/when, whether, multi-sentence)
4. Legal Context
5. Precise Question
6. Facts (specific, determinative)
7. Conclusion Not Assumed
8. Readability (subject/verb placement, punctuation)

Examples: The sample memos in Chapter 8 contain examples of questions presented and brief answers (see pages 145–46, 151–52).

Factual Background: Elaine Swift is severely allergic to eggs, wheat, and dairy products. She wanted to have a birthday party at Fun Zone. Fun Zone requires all birthday parties to include food purchases from Fun Zone and does not allow outside food. Elaine cannot eat any of Fun Zone's food because of her allergies, and Fun Zone would not change its policy to allow her to have her party there and bring in her own food.

Legal Background: The Americans with Disabilities Act (ADA) prohibits disability-based discrimination. It requires businesses to make reasonable accommodations for individuals with disabilities unless doing so would fundamentally alter the business. It is undisputed that Elaine's food allergies make her an individual with a disability under the ADA.

Legal Issue: Does Fun Zone's refusal to allow Elaine to bring in her own food violate the ADA?

Exercise: You have been asked to write a memo analyzing this legal issue. Below is a draft of a question presented on this issue written in the under/does/when format.

> Under the ADA, did Fun Zone, when it did not reasonably accommodate her disability, discriminate against Elaine?

a. Identify five specific problems with this question presented.

b. Rewrite the question presented in the under/does/when format and correct the identified problems.

c. Rewrite the question presented using the whether format and correct the identified problems.

d. Rewrite the question presented using the multi-sentence format and correct the identified problems.

Part B: Brief Answer

 Lightning Round

....

Skills Tested (explained on page 15):

1. Answer (short answer first, echo question language)
2. Conclusion-Rule-Application-Conclusion Format

....

Factual Background: Same as above.

Legal Background: Same as above.

Legal Issue: Same as above.

Exercise: Below is a draft of a brief answer to the question presented in Part A above:

> Fun Zone's policy against outside food is important to its business model as a dining and entertainment complex, and party food sales generate significant revenue. Thus, asking it to modify that policy is unreasonable. The ADA does not require businesses to make unreasonable changes.

a. Identify three specific problems with this brief answer.

b. Rewrite the brief answer and correct the identified problems.

Exercise 6

Part A: Question Presented

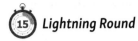 *Lightning Round*

....

Skills Tested (explained on pages 14–15):

1. Accepted Format (under/does/when)

2. Legal Context

3. Precise Question

4. Facts (specific, determinative, objective)

5. Readability (punctuation, conciseness)

....

Examples: The sample memos in Chapter 8 contain examples of questions presented and brief answers (see pages 145–46, 151–52).

Factual Background: At some point during a cross-country flight, Hazel Romero's wallet was stolen from the overhead storage area. There is no way to determine exactly when her wallet was taken. The flight took off in New York and landed in Los Angeles, and Los Angeles is in the Central District of California. Claire Grayson has been indicted for the theft, and the United States intends to prosecute her in the United States District Court for the Central District of California.

Legal Background: Federal Rule of Criminal Procedure 18 requires prosecution of crimes "in a district in which the offense was committed."

Legal Issue: Is venue proper in the United States District Court for the Central District of California?

Exercise: You are an intern in the prosecutor's office for the Central District of California, and you have been asked to write a memo analyzing this legal issue. The memo must include a question presented drafted in the under/does/when format. Below are three choices for each of the under/does/when components. Which one in each group is the best choice, based on the facts and law set out above? What is wrong with the other ones?

   I. <u>"Under" (Legal Context) Component</u>:

     A. Under FRCP 18,

     B. Under the federal venue rules,

     C. Under Federal Rule of Criminal Procedure 18, which requires prosecution of crimes in the district in which the offense was committed,

   II. <u>"Does" (Legal Question) Component</u>:

     A. is venue proper in the Central District of California

     B. can Grayson be prosecuted in the United States District Court for the Central District of California

     C. can a Central District of California jury convict Grayson of theft

  III. <u>"When" (Facts) Component</u>:

     A. when the plane landed in the Central District of California?

     B. when the district in which the air crime was committed cannot be determined but the plane landed in the Central District of California?

     C. when Ms. Grayson obviously stole Ms. Romero's wallet during the flight and so the wallet was stolen somewhere between New York, where the plane took off, and Los Angeles, where the plane landed, but no one knows exactly where?

Part B: Brief Answer

 *Lightning Round*

....

Skills Tested (explained on page 15):

1. Answer (short answer first, echo question language)
2. Conclusion-Rule-Application-Conclusion Format

....

Factual Background: Same as above.

Legal Background: Same as above.

Legal Issue: Same as above.

Exercise: The chart below contains sentences that could be part of the brief answer to the question presented in Part A above. For each sentence, first determine whether it should be included and explain your reasoning. Then, for the ones that should be included, determine in which order the sentences should appear.

BRIEF ANSWER SENTENCES
(1) The venue rule requires the United States to prosecute the defendant in the district in which the offense was committed.
(2) The plane landed in the Central District of California, so venue is proper there.
(3) No.
(4) The venue rule requires that a crime be prosecuted in the district in which the offense was committed.
(5) The prosecution cannot prove which district the plane was flying over at the time of the theft.
(6) Probably not.
(7) Venue is improper in the Central District of California.
(8) Thus, venue is probably not proper in the Central District of California because the prosecution cannot prove the crime was committed in that district.
(9) The venue rule requires a crime to be prosecuted where it happened.

Exercise 7

Part A: Question Presented

 *Deeper Dive*

Skills Tested (explained on pages 14–15):

1. Stands Alone
2. Accepted Format (under/does/when, whether, multi-sentence)
3. Legal Context
4. Precise Question
5. Facts (specific, determinative, objective)
6. Readability (subject/verb placement, punctuation, conciseness)

Examples: The sample memos in Chapter 8 contain examples of questions presented and brief answers (see pages 145–46, 151–52).

Legal Background: In Montana, a willful detention occurs when one directly restrains the physical liberty of another. A detention need not be express; if one inspires in a person a just fear of harm that renders the person incapable of exercising the free will to leave, then the person is detained.

Factual Background: Fred Hudson entered a Bigbox Corp. store to buy a gift for his cousin's birthday. He looked at several small clocks, picked one up and walked around with it, but ultimately left the clock on the shelf. As he exited the store, Hudson felt an arm on his shoulder. Hudson turned and saw a large security guard with a gun. The guard had his hand on the holstered gun as he spoke loudly to Hudson: "Stop. Come and let me check your pockets. If you don't follow me, you may never see your family again." Hudson looked at the gun and followed the guard. The guard placed Hudson in a small office, sat across from Hudson, and asked Hudson to empty his pockets. The door remained two inches open throughout the encounter. After twenty minutes, the guard released Hudson with an apology. "OK. You're clear. Sorry. We have to check."

Legal Issue: Did Bigbox Corp.'s security guard detain Fred Hudson?

Exercise: Draft a question presented in two different formats for the issue set out above.

Part B: Brief Answer

 *Deeper Dive*

....

Skills Tested (explained on page 15):

1. Answer (short answer first, echo question language)
2. Conclusion-Rule-Application-Conclusion Format

....

Legal Background: Same as above.

Factual Background: Same as above.

Legal Issue: Same as above.

Exercise: Draft a brief answer for the issue set out above.

Exercise 8

Part A: Question Presented

 *Deeper Dive*

Skills Tested (explained on pages 13–15):

1. Consistency (language, same format)
2. Stands Alone
3. Accepted Format (under/does/when, multi-sentence)
4. Legal Context
5. Precise Question
6. Facts (specific, determinative)
7. Readability (subject/verb placement, punctuation, conciseness)

Examples: The sample memos in Chapter 8 contain examples of questions presented and brief answers (see pages 145–46, 151–52).

Factual Background: The Lakes and the Bennetts are across-the-street neighbors in Monterey, California. The two families do not get along. When two FedEx boxes disappeared from the Lakes' porch while Mr. Lake was at work, he suspected Mr. Bennett had stolen them. To look for evidence that Bennett had stolen the packages, Lake used his binoculars to peer into Bennett's living room window, which was large, had no curtain, and faced the street. He saw Bennett eating dinner and watching television for several hours before Bennett caught Lake spying on him. Bennett sued Lake for invasion of privacy based on intrusion on seclusion.

Legal Background: Under California law, the elements of a claim for invasion of privacy based on intrusion on seclusion are (1) an intentional intrusion upon another's solitude, seclusion, or private affairs, which (2) would be highly offensive to a reasonable person. Private affairs include subject matter that an individual has a right to keep private. An intrusion is not highly offensive to a reasonable person if the person's expectation of privacy is unreasonable under the circumstances.

Legal Issue: Can Bennett establish the elements of invasion of privacy based on intrusion on seclusion?

Exercise: Write a question presented for each of the two elements of invasion of privacy based on intrusion on seclusion. Normally, a writer addressing two issues would use the same format for both of them. For the sake of practice in this exercise, however, write the first privacy element in the under/does/when format and write the second element in the multi-sentence format.

Part B: Brief Answer

 *Deeper Dive*

....

Skills Tested (explained on pages 13–15):

1. Consistency (language, same format, same order, number of questions and answers)
2. Answer (short answer first, echo question language)
3. Conclusion-Rule-Application-Conclusion Format

....

Factual Background: Same as above.

Legal Background: Same as above.

Legal Issue: Same as above.

Exercise: Write brief answers for each of the two questions presented in Part A above.

Chapter 4

Statement of Facts

Summary of Skills Tested

The legal memo's core mission is to answer a question by applying law to new facts. The statement of facts provides the factual framework for the analysis and conclusions reached in the memo. It tells the story of the case. In addition to basics such as concise and grammatically correct writing, several key skills strengthen this framework.

Fact Selection. Choosing which facts to include is the most fundamental skill in writing an effective statement of facts. All legally significant facts must be included. Be sure to include the facts that favor the client as well as those that do not. Every fact needed to analyze the case and reach a conclusion is legally significant. And if a fact is important enough to appear in the analysis section, it should also appear in the statement of facts. This way, the reader won't be surprised and can absorb the complete factual situation before seeing how the law is applied and the answer it yields.

SKILLS TESTED IN THIS CHAPTER	
SKILL	EXERCISE
Fact Selection	9, 10, 12, 13, 14, 15, 16
Structure	11, 12, 15, 16
Tone and Language	9, 10, 14, 16
Facts Only	10, 14
Party Descriptions	14

In addition, the statement of facts must contain the factual context necessary to understand the story and claims. This should generally include a very brief description of the parties. Key context facts may also include, for example, the relationship between the parties, the structure of a business, how a machine operates, the details of a medical procedure in a medical malpractice case, or the description of an intersection.

Even if not technically legally significant, important emotional facts should also be included, as they could influence a prediction on how a factfinder could decide the case. For example, a memo focused on the duty element of a negligence claim should still note that the plaintiff's face was severely burned, ending her lucrative modeling career.

If evidence from different sources conflicts, make sure to include all of it and point out the discrepancies.

Be thoughtful about how specifically to describe each fact. When details are provided, the reader assumes those details are important and will attempt to remember them. Make sure the details you include matter, so that the reader is not distracted by unimportant minutia. For example, the precise words a party or witness used may be crucial in analyzing intent or assessing how seemingly conflicting evidence might fit together. On the other hand, the color of a car involved in an accident may not matter if all parties to the accident are known.

Pay particular attention when giving dates. A specific date can provide the general time frame for the dispute, but other dates should be included only when the exact date adds important information. Other words and phrases—such as "the next day," "two weeks later," and "afterwards"—can show the passage of time without the need for a specific date.

Structure. To tell a compelling story and aid reader comprehension, facts should be arranged in a thoughtful, logical structure. To provide context, start with a brief orientation sentence or paragraph; end the statement of facts with a sentence that brings the reader up to date and transitions into the analysis that follows. Because most readers think chronologically, statements of facts tend to work best when structured in chronological order. Depart from chronological order only after careful thought in a particular circumstance, and then, consider whether a combination of chronological order and another format (such as explaining a topic) would be most helpful.

Once the overall structure is set, divide the statement of facts into paragraphs. Each paragraph should pertain to one portion of the overall story; use the topic sentence at the beginning of the paragraph to signal the paragraph's contents. To guide the reader from one paragraph to the next, use transitions at the beginning of the paragraph. Pointing words such as "this" or "that" within the paragraphs can also help clarify the narrative.

Be sure to integrate facts from different sources into a single coherent narrative rather than merely providing a witness-by-witness or document-by-document description.

Tone and Language. Keep the statement of facts balanced and objective. The memo is not an advocacy or persuasion piece; writing the facts to favor the client or any single perspective would thus be misguided. While a statement of facts may contain facts that are themselves tragic or dramatic, the author's tone should remain even-handed and professional. The memo writer should remain above the fray, avoiding a shocked, dramatic, or critical tone. Similarly, reject informal language, and do not base any assumptions on stereotypes about, for example, an actor's age, race, or gender. The facts should speak for themselves.

Facts Only. Include only facts, not inferences from facts, legal conclusions, or opinions. Inferences, conclusions, and opinions are arguments and should be saved for the analysis section. Facts are based on data, whereas inferences are based on assumptions. For example, this is a factual statement: Undercover officers staked out the front entrance of the building from 5:00 to 8:00 p.m., and during that time, no officer saw the defendant enter or exit the building. The following, by contrast, is an inference, because it depends on inferring an ultimate conclusion from the given facts: The defendant did not enter or exit the building from 5:00 to 8:00 p.m.

A statement of facts may properly describe a legal claim without including a legal conclusion. For example, saying that the plaintiff sued the defendant for negligence is appropriate, whereas a statement that the defendant was negligent is a legal conclusion that does not belong in the statement of facts.

Finally, the writer's opinion about a fact, such as whether it seems credible, is not a fact and should not be included.

Party Descriptions. Parties should be described using their names (last names usually preferred) or a descriptive term (like "the employer" or "the bank") rather than a procedural designation alone, such as plaintiff or defendant. Procedural designations are easily confused, while the goal is always to aid clarity and ease comprehension. If introducing the parties with their procedural designations, use their name and a procedural designation together to clarify their status (such as Plaintiff Anthony Cooper) on the first reference. After that, just use their names. If referring to the parties in the client's case, capitalize Plaintiff and Defendant, but otherwise use lower case.

In the exercises that follow, try your hand at the skills described above. In doing so, you will learn to present a complete, helpful, and lucid statement of facts. Remember to compare your answers with the annotated sample answers for the even-numbered problems included at the back of this volume. The two full sample memos in Chapter 8 contain statements of facts demonstrating these skills.

Exercise 9

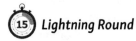 *Lightning Round*

Skills Tested (explained on pages 33–35):

1. Fact Selection (relevant details)
2. Tone and Language (objective)

Examples: The sample memos in Chapter 8 contain examples of statements of facts (see pages 146–47, 152–54).

Legal Principles: An employer is prohibited from firing an employee because the employee has reported the employer for engaging in an illegal activity. Whether the employer actually engaged in an illegal activity is irrelevant if the employee believes in good faith that the activity is illegal.

Legal Issue: Did Global fire Jan Carey because she reported that two Global vice presidents had made plans to steal from Global?

Exercise: Based on the legal principles governing this legal issue, remove the unnecessary facts and revise the wording to reflect an objective tone. For any facts you think are unnecessary, please explain your reasoning.

> Jan Carey has sued her former employer, Global, alleging that Global fired her in retaliation for reporting suspected illegal activity. Carey worked in Global's accounting department, and part of her job duties included ensuring compliance with state and federal ethics laws. She also prepared annual tax returns and helped formulate the annual budget. She had been performing this job for three years. After missing five days of work because she was deathly ill, Jan returned to work. As she was cleaning out a filing cabinet, she found notes used to prepare corporate tax returns from the last five years. She also found notes of discussions between two Global vice presidents of an intricate and devious scheme to steal $1 million from Global. Carey went to Human Resources and complained that she was overworked and asked for a new employee to be hired. She also reported the vice presidents' plans and turned over the documents she found. She was fired the next day, ostensibly for the ridiculous reason of violating Global's absence control policy for taking too many sick days. It turns out the notes were not in fact plans to steal but instead were ideas for a top-notch fiction thriller.

Exercise 10

 *Lightning Round*

....

> **Skills Tested (explained on pages 33–35):**
>
> 1. Fact Selection (relevant details)
> 2. Tone and Language (objective, not dramatic, no stereotypes)
> 3. Facts Only (no opinions)

....

Examples: The sample memos in Chapter 8 contain examples of statements of facts (see pages 146–47, 152–54).

Legal Principles:

1. A shopkeeper may detain a person reasonably suspected of theft.
2. The detention can last only a reasonable time and must be under reasonable conditions.

Exercise: The chart below contains some facts that a new associate has included in a draft statement of facts. Can you help the associate decide which facts should remain in the final version? If the fact should stay, note how it is relevant. If not, explain why. Does the language need revision to avoid unnecessary drama, slanting, or inappropriate stereotypes?

FACTS
(1) Our client, Mary Jones, is a sweet lady of seventy-five, who alleges that she was improperly detained while shopping at Big Buy, an electronics store.
(2) Jones was shopping for a new iPhone case for her niece.
(3) As she was comparing two iPhone cases, one slipped off the shelf and fell into her handbag.
(4) When Jones paid for one iPhone case and tried to leave the store, the security alarms went off.
(5) The store's tall and intimidating security guard grabbed Jones by the arm and pulled her into a windowless and prisonlike office near the front of the store.
(6) Other shoppers gathered in a mob near the office.
(7) After what seemed like an eternity, but was actually twenty minutes, the guard released Jones.

Exercise 11

 *Lightning Round*

Skill Tested (explained on page 34):

Structure (logical order, paragraphing, topic sentences, bridging words)

Examples: The sample memos in Chapter 8 contain examples of statements of facts (see pages 146–47, 152–54).

Legal Principles:

1. A person is generally under no duty to come to the aid of another person.

2. If a person promises to aid another and induces reliance or undertakes a course of action to assist another, then the person must fulfill the promise or carry out the course of action with reasonable care.

Exercise: Which of the following two statements of facts is more effective? Please state five specific reasons why.

Option A

One evening, friends Burt Livingston and Charlene Brewer went out to eat with two other friends. The waiter offered them a complimentary sample of battered puffer fish at the end of the meal. It is undisputed that the puffer fish would leave him with neurological damage. Three of the four friends declined, but Livingston took a large bite. Livingston said he felt as if he was flying, two minutes after he ate the puffer fish. The group decided to leave. They walked toward the door. While walking, Livingston suddenly clutched his stomach and then lay on the floor, immobile. One of the friends said she could take Livingston to the hospital right away. Brewer said that she lived closest to the hospital and would take Livingston for treatment. She said, "Don't you worry, guys. I got this." Livingston could not speak and could hardly move. Brewer drove Livingston to Brewer's apartment. She did not drive Livingston to the hospital. Livingston was almost unconscious. Brewer turned to him and said, "I'm feeling a bit tired. Just lie down and sleep it off." Both fell asleep. Livingston woke up at 10 a.m. and took the city bus to a local clinic. Burt Livingston is our client in a lawsuit, and he has filed a claim alleging that Defendant Charlene Brewer assumed a duty by assisting him when he was ill.

Option B

Our client, Plaintiff Burt Livingston, alleges that Defendant Charlene Brewer assumed a duty to him by assisting him when he was ill.

Livingston and his friend, Brewer, went out to eat with two other friends one evening. Toward the end of the meal, the waiter offered them a complimentary sample of battered puffer fish. Three of the four friends declined, but Livingston took a large bite. After two minutes, Livingston said he felt as if he was flying. The group then decided to leave. As they walked toward the door, Livingston suddenly clutched his stomach and then lay on the floor, immobile.

The friends discussed what they should do next. One of the friends said he could take Livingston to the ER right away. Brewer then said that she lived closest to the hospital and would take Livingston for treatment. She said, "Don't you worry, guys. I got this." Livingston could not speak and could hardly move.

Instead of driving to the hospital, Brewer drove to her own apartment. Livingston was almost unconscious. Brewer turned to him and said, "I'm feeling a bit tired. Just lie down and sleep it off." Both fell asleep. Livingston woke up at 10 a.m. and took the city bus to a local clinic. It is undisputed that the delay in treatment left Livingston with neurological damage.

Exercise 12

 *Lightning Round*

....

Skills Tested (explained on pages 33–34):

1. Fact Selection (dates and time indicators)
2. Structure (logical order, good flow)

....

Examples: The sample memos in Chapter 8 contain examples of statements of facts (see pages 146–47, 152–54).

Legal Principle: A person is liable for negligent entrustment if the person permits another to use a thing under the person's control if the person knows or should know that the other person is likely to use the thing in a manner that would cause an unreasonable risk of harm to others.

Exercise: Reorder these numbered sentences to present a chronological story. Edit the sentences to eliminate unnecessary dates and replace them with other time-indicating phrases as appropriate.

STATEMENT OF FACTS SENTENCES
(1) Thelma and Louise were long-time friends.
(2) Thelma asked Louise to borrow Louise's car on April 1, 2020, because her own car was in the repair shop and she needed to run an errand.
(3) Louise knew that Thelma had crashed into the bakery's front window on March 28, 2020, because she had gotten confused about the pedals, but she let Thelma borrow the car anyway.
(4) Thelma was declared legally blind in one eye on January 27, 2020, but Louise did not know this.
(5) Thelma had always been a good driver before she turned sixty on May 1, 2019.
(6) On March 28, 2020, Thelma drove up over the curb at her favorite bakery and into the bakery's front window when she mistook the gas pedal for the brake.
(7) While driving Louise's car on April 1, 2020, Thelma hit a young boy riding a bicycle, severely injuring him.

Exercise 13

⏱ (15) *Lightning Round*

....

Skill Tested (explained on pages 33–34):

Fact Selection (relevant details, negative facts, specificity)

....

Examples: The sample memos in Chapter 8 contain examples of statements of facts (see pages 146–47, 152–54).

Legal Principles:

1. In a medical malpractice suit, a doctor who acts outside the standard of care and whose actions proximately cause harm to another person is liable for the person's damages.

2. The standard of care is what a reasonably competent and skilled doctor would have done under similar circumstances.

Factual Background: Belinda Arcot has sued our client, Dr. Alana Green, for medical malpractice. This is a transcript of a statement Dr. Green gave shortly after the relevant incident.

> Poor Mrs. Arcot, I can't believe this happened. Hospital policy requires that all surgical instruments be sterilized three times, with each process being verified by a seal on the outside of the instrument packaging. It's my responsibility, as lead surgeon, to check for those seals before I operate. Belinda Arcot needed an emergency c-section, and in the rush, I just forgot to check the seals until after surgery. When I checked, I discovered that the instruments had only been sterilized twice. We monitored her closely for signs of infection, and sure enough, within a day, she developed an infection in the surgical site. We ended up having to perform a hysterectomy.

Exercise: Which of the following statements of facts is more effective? Please state five specific reasons why.

Option A

Belinda Arcot has sued our client, Dr. Alana Green, for medical malpractice, claiming Dr. Green used unsterile instruments while performing a c-section.

Hospital policy requires that all surgical instruments be sterilized three times before their use in an operation. Each step in the sterilization process is documented on a seal on the outside of the packaging. The lead surgeon must verify that all stages of the sterilization are complete before beginning any procedure.

Dr. Green performed an emergency c-section on Arcot but, based on her own admission, forgot to check the seals before the surgery. When Dr. Green checked afterwards, she discovered that the instruments had been sterilized only twice. Arcot's surgical wound became infected, and she eventually had to undergo a hysterectomy.

Option B

Dr. Green performed an emergency c-section on Mrs. Arcot but did not ensure that all hospital sanitation procedures were followed before surgery. Arcot suffered complications due to a post-surgical infection and has now sued Dr. Green for medical malpractice.

Exercise 14

 *Lightning Round*

....

Skills Tested (explained on pages 33–35):

1. Fact Selection (relevant details, specificity)
2. Tone and Language (not dramatic)
3. Facts Only (no opinions, no legal conclusions)
4. Party Descriptions

....

Examples: The sample memos in Chapter 8 contain examples of statements of facts (see pages 146–47, 152–54).

Legal Principle: A person who in good faith administers emergency care at the scene of an emergency or in a hospital is not liable in civil damages for those acts, except in the case of gross negligence.

Legal Issue: Is Charles Washington liable for gross negligence in attempting to treat Alan White's snake bite with a tourniquet?

Exercise: The following statement of facts contains bracketed alternative word choices. Please select the word or words that will be most helpful to the reader, bearing in mind the skills tested in this exercise. What is wrong with the other choices?

> *gives context*   *gives context*
>
> [Plaintiff] or [Plaintiff Alan White] is suing [Defendant] or [Defendant Charles Washington] for negligence based on Washington's [grossly negligent acts] or [actions] or [careless acts] after White suffered a snake bite during a camping trip. *not to conclusionary*
>
> White, a twenty-year-old college student, was camping [with Mary White, Susan White, Lila White, and Bob White, his family members] or [with his dear family] or [with his family] in Big Bend National Park when a [five-foot] or [large] or [large and extremely intimidating] snake bit him. *not too many words   not too many words* At the same time, Washington, a forty-year-old attorney, was hiking on a sandy trail when he heard screams coming from the nearby bushes. The screams were from White, [who had stepped on the snake] or [who had *no unnec. words* unfortunately stepped on the snake]. The [beautiful yet threatening snake suddenly struck him] or [snake struck him] or [snake struck him savagely].
>
> Washington ran over to White and tried to help. Washington had taken a first-aid class about thirty years earlier and thought he remembered how

Keep des Clewr

a snake bite should be treated. [**Defendant**] or [**Washington**] told White not to move a muscle, and Washington placed a tight tourniquet on White's leg. White immediately questioned whether a tourniquet was the right approach. White said, "I'm an Eagle Scout, and I know from my training that you should not place a tourniquet on a snake-bitten limb. Tourniquets can be very dangerous." Washington persisted, [**recklessly tightening**] or [**tightening**] or [**stubbornly tightening**] the tourniquet even further. After ten minutes, [**Plaintiff**] or [**plaintiff**] or [**White**] could not feel any sensation in his foot. White asked Washington again to remove the tourniquet; Washington [**seemed very confident**] or [**said he was "confident about the tourniquet"**] or [**acted in good faith**] and refused to remove it.

no unless ward s

not sure where corp s

gives de tayl

The tourniquet was so tight that it caused permanent injury. The snake bite itself caused no harm because the snake was nonvenomous and its teeth had barely grazed White's skin. [**White now claims that Washington's actions were grossly negligent.**] or [**Washington's actions were probably grossly negligent.**]

provdes dulim

Exercise 15

 *Deeper Dive*

Skills Tested (explained on pages 33–34):

1. Fact Selection (relevant details, negative facts, conflicting evidence, specificity)
2. Structure (logical order, paragraphing, good flow)

Examples: The sample memos in Chapter 8 contain examples of statements of facts (see pages 146–47, 152–54).

Legal Principle: An actor ordinarily has a duty to exercise reasonable care to avoid injuring another person when the actor's conduct creates a risk of physical harm to that person.

Factual Background: Trudy Vaughn has sued our client, Jerome Butler, for negligence arising out of an auto accident. Tiffany Smoak was a passenger in Mr. Butler's car at the time of the accident. Mr. Butler and Ms. Smoak provided the following witness statements:

> **Statement of Jerome Butler:**
>
> I was driving home after having dinner out with Tiffany when my car just suddenly crashed into another car after I went through the intersection at Walker and Main. That light was green. Me and Tiffany had been at dinner for at least three hours. I had two beers that whole time and I was 100% not drunk. I'm pretty sure the light was green. Tiffany was feeling a little sick, and I looked over at her a few times because I was worried she was about to throw up in my car.

> **Statement of Tiffany Smoak:**
>
> When Jerome crashed into that poor lady, I had my head down in my lap because I wasn't feeling so good, so I didn't really see what happened. I had three beers and two shots of whiskey when I was at dinner with Jerome. We hadn't seen each other in years, and it was fun to get a little drunk and catch up on old times. He was drinking with me, but he probably didn't drink as much as me, which is why we thought he should be the one driving. We were together at the restaurant for about two hours.

Exercise: Write a statement of facts segment combining these two witness statements. Focus particularly on including all determinative facts—both positive and negative—and stating the facts in an ordered structure. Make sure to account for the inconsistencies between the two witness statements. Your final product should be polished and flow well.

Exercise 16

 *Deeper Dive*

....

Skills Tested (explained on pages 33–35):

1. Fact Selection (relevant details, specificity)

2. Structure (logical order, paragraphing, topic sentences, bridging words, good flow)

3. Tone and Language (not dramatic)

....

Examples: The sample memos in Chapter 8 contain examples of statements of facts (see pages 146–47, 152–54).

Legal Principles:

1. A domestic animal, even if lost, is privately owned personal property. The captor of a lost animal does not acquire ownership of it unless the animal is abandoned. Property is abandoned if the owner intentionally gives up ownership.

2. A bailment contract, express or implied, is created when one person delivers personal property to another's possession in trust for a specific purpose, pursuant to an agreement that the owner will have the property returned to him or that the property will be accounted for or kept for the owner to reclaim it. In the case of a bailment, possession of the property is given to the bailee, but the original owner retains ownership of the property. Ownership is not transferred with possession of the property. A party who wrongfully sells or otherwise disposes of bailed property outside the bailment agreement has converted the property.

Legal Issue: Did the animal shelter breach its bailment agreement with Susan Johnson?

Exercise: The following paragraphs contain a narrative about a bailment agreement. Please complete the exercise in two steps. *Step 1:* Underline the facts that you plan to include in your statement of facts. *Step 2:* Arrange the facts into a set of carefully constructed paragraphs. Be sure to begin with an orientation sentence that explains the matter's context. Conclude with a sentence that brings the reader up to date and thus transitions into the rest of the memo.

Our client, Susan Johnson, lived in Miami, Florida, with her two children and her beloved and gentle rescue terrier, Gizmo. As a hurricane approached, the dog would not fit in the car as they tried to evacuate. *[handwritten]*

The hurricane gathered strength and continued on track toward Miami; Johnson struggled with her options. Johnson remembered a local shelter, the Pet Friends Emergency Pet Shelter, and she took Gizmo to the intake office. "I just need help until the hurricane passes," Johnson said. "OK," said the shelter manager. "We can take him. Just wait until at least two days after the hurricane to come and get him. Make sure you're back within fifteen days from now, or we will adopt him out. There's a $20 hurricane shelter fee for this."

"Please take care of him. Gizmo, baby, I love you. Be safe." The shelter manager looked at the form. "Looks good," she said. Johnson paid the $20 fee, kissed Gizmo on the nose, and watched as he was led away to the kennels. Johnson quickly returned to her apartment and continued to gather her belongings for the evacuation. She traveled two hundred miles north to a small hotel and waited with her children.

The following day, the storm hit. Johnson's apartment was severely damaged. She looked online for an undamaged apartment, but there were few choices, especially for a larger dog like Gizmo. She called the Pet Friends shelter intending to update the staff on her situation, but the line was always busy.

After the storm, the shelter's files became disorganized, and the regular file clerk quit due to her family's problems with the storm. Gizmo stayed at the shelter for a week after the storm, but then he became separated from his file, and the shelter manager decided he should be adopted out. At the same time Gizmo was adopted out, Johnson finally found an apartment willing to take the family and Gizmo too. She quickly learned, however, that Gizmo had been adopted by another family. She now wants to enforce the bailment agreement and to challenge the new adoption contract on the basis of mutual mistake.

[handwritten margin note: good paragraphs]

Chapter 5

Discussion

In the discussion section, the writer states the initial conclusion, lays out the law in detail, and shows how the law applies to the client's facts. Next, the writer sets out a counterargument, developing that argument and then promptly rebutting it. The rebuttal should show exactly why the writer's conclusion, also called the affirmative argument, prevails. A final conclusion completes the discussion section. The following parts make up the discussion section; each one is explained in greater detail in the pertinent sub-chapter's Summary of Skills Tested. The exercises then go on to test the specific skills.

A. Roadmap. When a discussion section addresses more than one issue, the writer should alert the reader to the content ahead. The mechanism for doing so is a roadmap. The roadmap usually contains the issue's conclusion, the overall rule, and a short basis for the conclusion.

B. Discussion Conclusions. The discussion of each specific issue begins with a conclusion. Whenever possible, the writer should briefly give the basis for the conclusion. The discussion section will end with a conclusion as well, setting out the final conclusion with a reason, in language substantively consistent with, but not identical to, the opening conclusion.

C. Rule and Explanation. Next, the rule sets out the law relevant to the issue, without reference to the client's facts. The rule progresses from broad statements of law to narrower ones, beginning with the highest authority. The rule's narrower points should be tailored so that they are relevant and useful to the specific analysis that follows.

Then, the explanation further sets out the law, adding more detail and explaining how the law applies under particular circumstances. The explanation should lay out the relevant case law in the manner most effective for the particular issue. The writer can use parenthetical statements or complete case illustrations when those would be helpful.

D. Application. In the application, the writer makes a clear shift to the current issue and sets out the thesis for the affirmative argument. The thesis contains the overall conclusion and summarizes the arguments to follow. The application follows a clear structure, using separate argument points as topic sentences for the paragraphs that follow. To support the arguments, the writer should use rule-based reasoning, analogical reasoning, or a combination of the two. Effective analogies should contain specific, relevant comparisons to parallel facts or reasoning in the precedent cases. The writer should explicitly state the inference to be drawn from any comparisons, referring back to the rule and clearly concluding each argument point.

E. Counterargument and Rebuttal. The writer can intersperse countervailing considerations throughout the affirmative argument. The main counterargument, however, should follow the affirmative argument. To avoid confusion, the counterargument begins with a clear shift to the main argument's opposing side, then develops the argument using law and facts, as appropriate. The writer should immediately rebut the counterargument, again using specifics. The rebuttal should avoid a bare repetition of the affirmative argument.

In each section that follows, you will find a detailed explanation of the skills required to write that part of the discussion effectively. You can use the exercises in each section to practice the skills. To see examples of these memo sections and to understand how they fit together, turn to the annotated sample memos in Chapter 8. One memo addresses a single issue and the other addresses two.

Roadmap

Summary of Skills Tested

A roadmap (sometimes called the umbrella, overall paragraph, introduction paragraph, or thesis paragraph) is useful at the beginning of a discussion section that covers more than one issue or at the beginning of any section that contains subsections. The roadmap is the reader's first opportunity to grasp the discussion section's full scope and context; it sets the reader's expectations for what is to come. A helpful roadmap gives the conclusion on all issues, provides the legal context, previews the discussion's structure, and then follows with the additional components set out below.

SKILLS TESTED IN THIS CHAPTER	
SKILL	EXERCISE
Conclusion	17, 18
Legal Background	17, 18
Memo Contents	17, 18
Nuts and Bolts	17, 18

Conclusion. The roadmap's conclusion must cover all points that the discussion addresses. This way, the reader knows the complete answer up front. Whenever possible, the conclusion should include a brief summary of the key reasons for the conclusion.

Legal Background. The roadmap provides the memo's legal context. Typically, that would include the overall rule for each issue. Even if the discussion section only addresses some elements of a claim, the roadmap should still set out the entire rule so the reader can understand the context. If, however, a memo addresses more than one unrelated issue and providing the overall rule for each issue would produce an ungainly roadmap, you can save the overall rules for the rule section. Also, if there are important policy considerations that guide the entire discussion, the roadmap is a good place to set out such points. Be sure to include citations to support the law.

Memo Contents. The roadmap tells the reader what to expect in the discussion section. If the memo does not include all elements of the claim set out in the overall rule, the roadmap should so state and explain why. If an element is excluded from the discussion because it is easily met, the roadmap should briefly explain that. The roadmap should also show how elements in the discussion section fit together (for example, if the issues discussed build on one another or if they are independent alternatives).

Nuts and Bolts. The roadmap should not include issue-specific details, as that would unnecessarily duplicate information found later in the discussion. Rather, the roadmap provides only necessary context and orientation. Finally, ensure that the roadmap follows the discussion's structure; this provides a sense of flow and organization, allowing the reader to learn what lies ahead.

Using the following exercises, try your hand at applying the points set out above. You can check your work using the even-numbered annotated sample exercises at the back of this book. The two-issue sample memo in Chapter 8 contains an example of a roadmap.

Exercise 17

 *Lightning Round*

Skills Tested (explained on pages 51–52):

1. Conclusion (comprehensive, reasoning explained)
2. Legal Background (overall rule, legal context)
3. Memo Contents (included items, relationship between items)
4. Nuts and Bolts (no issue-specific material, order follows memo structure)

Example: The two-issue sample memo in Chapter 8 contains an example of a roadmap (see page 154).

Factual Background: Ana Katic is the mother of L.K., a two-year-old girl. Katic played the piano with a traveling jazz band. Katic traveled with L.K. on a two-month musical tour because Katic had no other childcare. During the tour, Katic tried to keep L.K. separate from the band members due to their loud parties and drug use. Still, on two occasions, other band members used drugs around L.K. During a two-day period in which the band had no time to grocery shop, L.K. had only gummy bears and French fries to eat. After the tour, however, Katic set up a stable home, took parenting classes, and taught music lessons at an after-school program. L.K. and Katic are affectionate to one another and are happy together. The State learned of the drug use and poor diet on the road and may begin parental termination proceedings.

Legal Background: A court may order termination of the parent-child relationship if it finds by clear and convincing evidence that (1) the parent has engaged in conduct that endangers the physical or emotional well-being of the child and (2) termination is in the child's best interest. Tex. Fam. Code Ann. § 161.001(b)(1)(E), (b)(2).

Legal Issue: Will a court terminate Ana Katic's parental rights based on these two elements?

Exercise: Please decide which sentences belong in a roadmap for a memo on this two-element legal issue; explain your reasoning. Then combine the sentences in the correct order so they create an appropriate roadmap.

ROADMAP SENTENCES
(1) The natural right that exists between parents and their children is one of constitutional dimension, and there is a strong presumption that a child's best interest is served by preservation of parents' rights. *In re G.M.*, 596 S.W.2d 846, 846 (Tex. 1980).
(2) The court cannot terminate Katic's parental rights.
(3) The court probably will not terminate Katic's parental rights because Katic worked to ensure her child's safety and the two enjoy a strong parent-child relationship.
(4) Katic probably did not engage in endangering conduct because she tried to ensure her child's safety and later provided a more stable home. Termination probably is not in L.K.'s best interest because Katic and L.K. enjoy a strong relationship, and Katic is working toward being a better parent. Thus, a court probably will not terminate Katic's parental rights.
(5) A court may order termination of the parent-child relationship if it finds by clear and convincing evidence that (1) the parent has engaged in conduct that endangers the physical or emotional well-being of the child and (2) termination is in the child's best interest. Tex. Fam. Code Ann. § 161.001(b)(1)(E), (b)(2).
(6) Just as the court did not terminate the parent's rights in *Florey* due to reckless endangerment, neither should the court here.

Exercise 18

 *Lightning Round*

....

Skills Tested (explained on pages 51–52):

1. Conclusion (comprehensive, reasoning explained)

2. Legal Background (overall rule, legal context)

3. Memo Contents (excluded items, included items, relationship between items)

4. Nuts and Bolts (no issue-specific material, order follows memo structure)

....

Example: The two-issue sample memo in Chapter 8 contains an example of a roadmap (see page 154).

Factual Background: Johnny Hudson worked for Mr. Burger, a fast-food chain, taking orders and serving food. Austin Parks, a Mr. Burger customer, became upset when he did not have his food ten minutes after placing his order. Parks started berating Hudson, who was working behind the counter and had taken Parks's order. Hudson responded by throwing a milkshake blender at Parks, hitting him in the head. Parks has sued Hudson and Mr. Burger.

Legal Background: Tort law generally imposes no liability on one person for the conduct of another. *Wisenhouse v. Armendez*, 14 S.W.3d 200, 201 (Tex. App. 2000). An exception exists in the employment context, where an employer can be held vicariously liable for a worker's tortious conduct if the worker was an employee acting in the course and scope of employment at the time of the tort. *Id.* A worker is an employee if the employer exercises sufficient control over the methods, details, and operations of the worker's job. *Id.* An employee acts in the course and scope of employment if the action is taken to further the employer's interest and not based on personal animosity. *Id.*

Legal Issue: Will Mr. Burger be vicariously liable for Hudson's assault on Parks?

Exercise: Is Option A or Option B the better version of a roadmap paragraph for a memo analyzing this issue? Identify seven specific reasons why.

Option A

A court will probably conclude that Hudson was not acting in the course and scope of his employment when he assaulted Parks. An exception provides that employers can be vicariously liable for a worker's tort if the worker is (1) an employee, (2) acting in the course and scope of employment, (3) at the time of the tortious conduct. A worker is an employee if the employer exercises sufficient control over the methods, details, and operations of the worker's job. An employee acts in the course and scope of employment if the action is taken to further the employer's interest and not based on personal animosity. This memo will therefore not address the third element regarding timing. It will address whether Hudson was acting in the course and scope of employment when he assaulted Parks and whether Hudson was an employee.

Option B

Mr. Burger will probably not be vicariously liable for Hudson's assault on Parks; although Hudson was most likely Mr. Burger's employee, he was probably not acting in the course and scope of his employment when he assaulted Parks. Tort law generally imposes no liability on one person for another's conduct. *Wisenhouse v. Armendez*, 14 S.W.3d 200, 201 (Tex. App. 2000). An exception provides that employers can be vicariously liable for a worker's tort if the worker is (1) an employee, (2) acting in the course and scope of employment, (3) at the time of the tortious conduct. *Id.* Hudson was on shift working for Mr. Burger when he threw the milkshake blender at Parks, and thus the timing element is not an issue. This memo will therefore address whether Hudson was an employee at the time of the assault and, if so, whether he was acting in the course and scope of his employment when he assaulted Parks. Hudson was most likely a Mr. Burger employee because Mr. Burger controlled all essential details of Hudson's work. Because Hudson acted out of anger and not to further Mr. Burger's business, however, Hudson was probably not acting in the course and scope of his employment, and thus Mr. Burger will probably not be vicariously liable for his conduct.

Discussion Conclusions

Summary of Skills Tested

The discussion section's introductory and final conclusions provide the writer's bottom-line answer and frame the discussion. A deft introductory conclusion sets the tone for a skillful analysis; a complete final conclusion rounds out the discussion and signals that the analysis is complete. Though including both introductory and final conclusions may seem repetitive, the two serve distinct functions. Your reader will appreciate initial and final conclusions that incorporate the following skills.

Answer the Question. An initial conclusion must answer the precise question asked. When, for example, the question is whether a particular duty exists, the writer may be tempted to answer more broadly about the entire claim's chance of success. The writer should, however, confine the conclusion to the particular issue that the assigning person has framed. The initial conclusion should also provide a sense of the writer's confidence in that outcome.

SKILLS TESTED IN THIS CHAPTER	
SKILL	EXERCISE
Answer the Question	19, 20
Give a Reason When Possible	19, 20
Keep It Short	20
Consistency	19, 20

Give a Reason When Possible. The writer should, whenever possible, accompany the predicted outcome with a thumbnail sketch of the underlying reasoning. Some legal issues may be so complicated that a summary answer would be ungainly, detracting from the conclusion's clarity and concision. In that situation, a bare predictive conclusion is also acceptable.

Keep It Short. Each conclusion is traditionally written in a single sentence. Where the legal issue is complicated and the conclusion cannot be written in one sentence, the writer can use two. To be effective, however, the conclusions and the underlying reasons should be as succinct as possible. Citations should not be included because they increase the length without adding value, given that the citations will be included in the rules and analysis immediately between the two conclusions.

Consistency. Though the introductory and final conclusions will contain the same information, it is important to know what language should be repeated and what should be varied. The reader will never want to read the exact same sentence twice. The two conclusions should contain consistent substantive language but varied non-substantive language and sentence structure. For example, the key words from a rule should be the same in both.

It is particularly important to keep the prediction language consistent. The conclusion will carry forward the predictive conclusion first found in the memo's introduction and brief answer. If the brief answer states, for example, that a particular outcome to an issue is almost certain, then each conclusion within the memo should be equally confident. The memo's substantive legal answer is fixed at the memo's outset, and any subsequent variation would be confusing and incorrect.

In the following exercises, you can work on the skills needed for complete and informative conclusions. You will find annotated sample answers for the even-numbered problems at the back of this volume. Chapter 8 contains sample memos demonstrating how to write conclusions for the discussion section.

Exercise 19

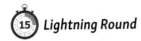 *Lightning Round*

....

Skills Tested (explained on pages 57–58):

1. Answer the Question
2. Give a Reason When Possible
3. Consistency (vary wording but not substance, consistent prediction language)

....

Examples: The sample memos in Chapter 8 contain examples of introductory and final conclusions for the discussion section (see pages 147, 150, 154, 157, 159).

Legal Background: A physician-patient relationship is required for a medical malpractice claim; the relationship can be inferred from the acts and conduct of the parties. An on-call physician without a prior relationship to the patient may assume a duty if the physician takes some affirmative action such as evaluating the information provided and making a medical decision toward treating the patient. A referral to another physician does not, without more, create a physician-patient relationship.

Legal Issue: Did a physician-patient relationship arise between on-call physician Dr. Antonio and patient Maria Navarro?

Exercise: The following are three introductory conclusions and three final conclusions in the discussion section of a memo on this issue. Which introductory conclusion is more effective? Which final conclusion is more effective? Please give specific reasons for your answers.

continued

Introductory Conclusions:

(1) To establish a physician-patient relationship, one has to take affirmative actions to treat, which Dr. Antonio did not do.

(2) Maria Navarro cannot bring a medical malpractice lawsuit against Dr. Antonio.

(3) A physician-patient relationship probably does not exist between Dr. Antonio and Maria Navarro because Dr. Antonio did not act affirmatively to treat Navarro but only listened to symptoms and suggested that Navarro see another physician.

Final Conclusions:

(1) Dr. Antonio's actions were not affirmative acts to treat the patient, so Dr. Antonio did not establish a physician-patient relationship.

(2) Dr. Antonio's actions probably did not amount to affirmative acts to treat the patient, so Dr. Antonio probably did not establish a physician-patient relationship.

(3) Maria Navarro cannot bring a medical malpractice claim against Dr. Antonio because Dr. Antonio did not establish a physician-patient relationship.

Exercise 20

 *Lightning Round*

....

Skills Tested (explained on pages 57–58):

1. Answer the Question

2. Give a Reason When Possible

3. Keep It Short

4. Consistency (vary wording but not substance, consistent prediction
   language)

....

Examples: The sample memos in Chapter 8 contain examples of introductory and final conclusions for the discussion section (see pages 147, 150, 154, 157, 159).

Legal Background: South Carolina law requires a party offering blood evidence to establish, at least as far as practicable, a complete chain of custody, tracing possession from the time the specimen is taken from the human body to the final analysis. *S.C. Dep't of Soc. Servs. v. Cochran*, 614 S.E.2d 642, 646 (S.C. 2005). The court will generally uphold the chain of custody if the safeguards used ensure the integrity of the evidence. *Id.*

Legal Issue: Will the State be able to sufficiently establish the chain of custody of the client's blood sample, which showed a blood alcohol content over the legal driving limit?

Exercise: The following are the introductory and final conclusions in the discussion section of a memo on this issue. Identify five problems with this set of conclusions.

continued

Introductory Conclusion: The blood test is likely admissible, *see S.C. Dep't of Soc. Servs. v. Cochran*, 614 S.E.2d 642, 646 (S.C. 2005), because even though the officer stored the blood sample in his trunk for two days before taking it to the evidence locker, no one else had access to his car during that time because it was locked in his garage and his wife was out of town, the evidence bag he stored the sample in showed no signs of tampering, and the officer testified that the blood sample appeared to be in the same condition when he removed it from his trunk as when he placed it inside, and therefore the chain of custody can be established.

Final Conclusion: A court might find that the chain of custody can be established as far as practicable.

Rule and Explanation

Summary of Skills Tested

The legal memo answers a question by applying relevant law to the facts at hand. Thus, the relevant law is the memo's foundation. To craft an effective memo, the legal writer must explain the law in an accurate, lucid, and concise manner, so the reader understands and trusts the writer's legal conclusions. To describe the law, a legal writer sets out two parts: the rule and explanation. The rule itself is a statement of the law, without reference to the facts of particular cases. Unless the rule is very straightforward, additional explanation follows. This explanation can be in one of several different forms, ranging from brief to more extensive. These aspects of the rule and explanation are described below, together with other pointers for an effective rule and explanation.

Rule Contours. A useful and accurate rule statement depends first on the choice of authority. The writer should of course prefer binding, primary authority, starting with any relevant statutes and followed by case law from the highest pertinent court.

The rule should begin with broader statements of the law, progressing to more specific and narrow aspects. As the rule progresses from broad to narrow, make sure each aspect of your rule is tailored to apply to the specific issue. The goal is not to provide a general statement of the law but to include only the rules and subrules directly applicable in the case. In a burglary case, for

SKILLS TESTED IN THIS CHAPTER	
SKILL	EXERCISE
Rule Contours	21, 22, 24, 25, 27, 28, 29, 30, 32
Treatment Depth	26, 29, 30
Case Illustration	23, 24, 27, 30, 31, 32
Multiple Case Illustrations	31
Nuts and Bolts	21, 23, 24, 25, 27, 30, 31, 32

example, a barn might under certain circumstances be considered a "habitation" for purposes of that rule; this observation fits well in the rule where the memo concerns a burglary that took place in a barn. The same point would be superfluous, however, where the burglary unequivocally occurred in a house. The legal reader assumes that all content in a legal memo is significant, so the inclusion of unneeded law not only wastes time but sows confusion.

At the same time, the legal writer must include all rules that will be expanded in a case illustration or discussed in the analysis section. The rule should set out a complete framework of the law, which is then developed in the explanation and analysis. A reader should not be surprised with new rules in a case illustration or in the analysis.

Treatment Depth. Once the rule is in place, the legal writer must decide how much more explanation of the law the reader needs. If the rule is simple and its application straightforward, the writer can stop there. More often, though, the reader will want to see at least some explanation of how the rule functions in particular cases. The writer can choose from several different techniques to explain the law, ranging from the briefest, which is a parenthetical explanation following a citation, to the most detailed, which is a full case illustration, containing a case's relevant legal principles, facts, and reasoning. If the writer seeks a middle ground, a short explanation will suffice. The choice will depend on many factors, such as the legal issue's complexity, whether the issue is fact-intensive and is thus suitable for comparison to factually similar cases, whether any factually similar cases exist, and any space constraints for the document.

Case Illustration. The case illustration follows the rule; it is a deeper exploration of a single, carefully selected case that further illuminates a rule you have already stated in the rule paragraph. Through a case illustration, the reader can understand how the court applied the law to particular facts and the reasoning that drove the court's conclusion. This can in turn elucidate how the law might apply to the facts at hand. Note that while this book uses the term "case illustration," the same concept may equally be called the "rule illustration," "rule proof," or "precedent" portion of the discussion.

The case illustration begins with a sentence that highlights the case's relevance to the issue. This introductory sentence functions as the thesis sentence of the case illustration paragraph. The introductory sentence can, for example, consist of a pertinent statement of law from the case. Or, it can encapsulate the issue's outcome and state a few of the most telling determinative facts. In any event, the opening sentence should do more than merely repeat a rule from the rule paragraph.

After that, the case illustration explains all the relevant case facts. Relevant facts are those that control the court's decision as well as any context facts necessary for the reader's understanding. Avoid discussing procedural issues except where strictly relevant.

The court's reasoning generally follows the facts; the holding then rounds out the case illustration. Both the court's holding and reasoning must be included in every case illustration.

A case illustration must be tailored to the specific issue in the case. A case illustration is not a case brief, in which the writer attempts to explain all key aspects of a case. Rather, a case illustration should be carefully—but accurately—cropped to focus the reader only on the portion of the case that will be relevant to the analysis that follows.

Multiple Case Illustrations. Where a memo requires multiple case illustrations to explain the law, the writer should set them out thoughtfully, using transitions to show their relationship. By ending the first case illustration with the court's holding, the writer can then use a transition such as "similarly" or "in contrast" to set the reader's expectations in regard to the cases' relationship to one another.

Nuts and Bolts. As you craft your rule and explanation, note the following additional requirements and conventions. Be sure to cite your source after each sentence. After all, the rule and explanation are the bedrock of your memo, and your citations both assure the reader that your conclusions are based on good law and allow the reader to refer to your sources.

Do not include client facts in your rule and explanation sections—you may be tempted to do so because your rule and explanation must be written with the client facts in mind. But the client facts themselves do not belong in the explanation and should appear only after the reader fully understands the law.

Quote only sparingly from your source statutes and cases. The reader expects you to present and explain the law in a palatable fashion. Large chunks of quoted text are unappealing and hard to digest, although a carefully selected phrase or sentence—particularly from an applicable statute or controlling case—is often helpful.

Finally, write the case illustrations in past tense. These cases took place in the past, so past tense will seem more natural for your explanation.

As you work through the exercises, refer to the annotated sample answers in the back of this volume for the even-numbered problems. You can see samples of rule and explanation paragraphs in the memos provided in Chapter 8.

Exercise 21

 *Lightning Round*

Skills Tested (explained on pages 63–65):

1. Rule Contours (broad to narrow)

2. Nuts and Bolts (citations)

Examples: The sample memos in Chapter 8 contain examples of rule and explanation paragraphs (see pages 147–49, 154–55, 157–58).

Legal Principles:

> Ga. Code Ann. § 51-7-20: False imprisonment is the unlawful detention of another, for any length of time, whereby such person is deprived of his personal liberty.
>
> *Smith v. Wal-Mart Stores E., LP*, 765 S.E.2d 518, 522 (Ga. Ct. App. 2014): The essential elements of the cause of action for false imprisonment are a detention of another for any length of time and the unlawfulness of that detention. A detention need not consist of physical restraint, but may arise out of words, acts, gestures, or the like, which induce a reasonable apprehension that force will be used if the plaintiff does not submit; and it is sufficient if they operate upon the will of the person threatened, and result in a reasonable fear of personal difficulty or personal injuries.

Exercise: Based on these two authorities, is Option A or Option B the better formulation of a rule? Give specific reasons for your answer.

Option A

The Georgia Code defines false imprisonment as an unlawful detention of another, where the person is "deprived of his personal liberty" for any length of time. Ga. Code Ann. § 51-7-20. A detention may be physical, but can also arise out of words, gestures, or other actions that give rise to a reasonable belief that force will be used if the plaintiff does not submit. *Smith v. Wal-Mart Stores E., LP*, 765 S.E.2d 518, 522 (Ga. Ct. App. 2014). If the defendant's actions operate on the will of the plaintiff and result in a reasonable fear of "personal difficulty or personal injuries," then the person is considered detained. *Id.*

Option B

A detention may be physical, but can also arise out of words, gestures, or other actions that give rise to a reasonable belief that force will be used if the plaintiff does not submit. *Smith v. Wal-Mart Stores E., LP*, 765 S.E.2d 518, 522 (Ga. Ct. App. 2014). If a defendant's actions operate on the will of a plaintiff and result in a reasonable fear of "personal difficulty or personal injuries," then the person is considered detained. The Georgia Code defines false imprisonment as an unlawful detention of another, where the person is "deprived of his personal liberty" for any length of time. Ga. Code Ann. § 51-7-20.

Exercise 22

 *Lightning Round*

....

Skill Tested (explained on pages 63–64):

Rule Contours (choice of authority, rule tailoring)

....

Examples: The sample memos in Chapter 8 contain examples of rule and explanation paragraphs (see pages 147–49, 154–55, 157–58).

Factual Background: Your client, Leslie Brenner, was held handcuffed in a locked office in a Bullseye department store, based on the suspicion that she had stolen some sunglasses. After three minutes passed, the manager removed the handcuffs and opened the door. He told Brenner that she could leave if she wanted to, but if she wanted to avoid incarceration, she had better stay. Brenner has made a claim for false imprisonment. Bullseye plans to make two arguments: (1) that Brenner was not detained during the first three minutes because such a short a detention should not be considered an actionable detention at all and (2) that Brenner was not detained after the manager removed the handcuffs.

Legal Principles:

> Ga. Code Ann. § 51-7-20: False imprisonment is the unlawful detention of another, for any length of time, whereby such person is deprived of his personal liberty.
>
> *Smith v. Wal-Mart Stores E., LP*, 765 S.E.2d 518, 522 (Ga. Ct. App. 2014): An essential element of the cause of action for false imprisonment is a detention of another for any length of time. A detention need not consist of physical restraint, but may arise out of words, acts, gestures, or the like, which induce a reasonable apprehension that force will be used if the plaintiff does not submit; it is sufficient if they operate upon the will of the person threatened and result in a reasonable fear of personal difficulty or personal injuries.
>
> *Taylor v. Madison Stores*, 785 S.E.2d 718, 720 (Ga. Ct. App. 2016): Even if a detention lasts only a second, a liberty interest is still implicated because a person does not have the right to detain another. Here, the plaintiff was held for two minutes, sufficient time for the claim to survive summary judgment on the basis of time.

> *Trevino v. Macie's Stores*, 830 S.E.2d 318, 320 (Ga. Ct. App. 2019):
> A person is detained if the person is made to believe that departing
> would result in incarceration, even if the person has a clear physical
> path to the exit.

Exercise: Each one of the above authorities includes rule language that pertains
to false imprisonment. Based on these authorities, which one of the four options
below is the best formulation of the rule to address Bullseye's first argument? Which
one is the best for its second argument? Why? Keep in mind that the rule should be
relevant to the overall point, so focus carefully on the precise issue for each argument.

Option A

> False imprisonment is the unlawful detention of another, where
> the person is "deprived of his personal liberty." Ga. Code Ann.
> § 51-7-20. A detention may be physical, but can also arise out of
> words, gestures, or other actions that give rise to a reasonable belief
> that force will be used if the plaintiff does not submit. *Smith v. Wal-
> Mart Stores E., LP*, 765 S.E.2d 518, 522 (Ga. Ct. App. 2014). If the
> defendant's actions operate on the will of the plaintiff and result in
> a reasonable fear of "personal difficulty or personal injuries," then
> the person is considered detained. *Id.*

Option B

> False imprisonment is an unlawful detention of another, where
> the person is "deprived of his personal liberty" for any length of time.
> Ga. Code Ann. § 51-7-20. Even if a person is held for the briefest
> amount of time, the person's liberty is still at stake and the detention
> meets the statutory length of time requirement. *Taylor v. Madison
> Stores*, 785 S.E.2d 718, 720 (Ga. Ct. App. 2016).

continued

Option C

False imprisonment is the unlawful detention of another, where the person is "deprived of his personal liberty." Ga. Code Ann. § 51-7-20. A detention may be physical but can also arise out of words, gestures, or other actions that give rise to a reasonable belief that force will be used if the plaintiff does not submit. *Smith v. Wal-Mart Stores E., LP*, 765 S.E.2d 518, 522 (Ga. Ct. App. 2014). If the defendant's actions operate on the will of the plaintiff and result in a reasonable fear of "personal difficulty or personal injuries," then the person is considered detained. *Id.* A person is detained if the person is made to believe that incarceration would result from departure, even if the person is physically able to leave. *Trevino v. Macie's Stores*, 830 S.E.2d 318, 320 (Ga. Ct. App. 2019).

Option D

False imprisonment is the unlawful detention of another, where the person is "deprived of his personal liberty." Ga. Code Ann. § 51-7-20. If the defendant's actions operate on the will of the plaintiff and result in a reasonable fear of "personal difficulty or personal injuries," then the person is considered detained. *Id.* A person is detained if the person is made to believe that incarceration would result from departure, even if the person is physically able to leave. *Trevino v. Macie's Stores*, 830 S.E.2d 318, 320 (Ga. Ct. App. 2019).

Exercise 23

 *Lightning Round*

....

Skills Tested (explained on pages 64–65):

1. Case Illustration (introductory sentence, fact selection, reasoning and holding)
2. Nuts and Bolts (citations)

....

Examples: The sample memos in Chapter 8 contain examples of rule and explanation paragraphs (see pages 147–49, 154–55, 157–58).

Factual Background: Your client is charged with robbing a store while pointing to his Swiss Army knife. He did not open or brandish the knife, but he pointed to the knife when he demanded the money. You are analyzing whether the Swiss Army knife, when so used, can be deemed a "deadly weapon" and thus give rise to additional criminal charges.

Exercise: You have found a case addressing the deadly weapon issue in the context of a hunting knife that was partially unsheathed during a robbery. Because the case is rather similar to yours, you have decided to include a full case illustration of the case in your memo.

Put the following numbered parts of the case illustration in the most useful order. Cite appropriately after each sentence, using the following citation: *Billey v. State*, 45 S.W.3d 34 (Tex. 2017). Each paragraph is followed by the page number on which the information appears.

continued

(1) The court reasoned that although there was no express threat, the partial exposure of the knife and statement that the defendant "wasn't kidding" presented an implied threat of injury—there was no other reason to show a knife during the robbery. Whether or not the defendant actually intended to carry out the threat, the threat had its desired effect in that the victim handed over the money. In addition, the defendant was close enough to the victim to carry out the threat. Page 35.

(2) The knife was therefore considered a deadly weapon. Page 40.

(3) In that case, the defendant was in the course of robbing a store when the victim asked if he was "kidding" about the robbery. In response, the defendant said he "wasn't kidding" and pointed to a partially unsheathed knife in his pocket. The victim testified that she was afraid of the knife because there was no reason to carry a knife into a store during a robbery except to hurt someone. Page 37.

(4) A weapon was considered a deadly weapon where the defendant made an implied threat and showed a partially unsheathed hunting knife during a robbery. Page 39.

Exercise 24

 *Lightning Round*

Skills Tested (explained on pages 63–65):

1. Rule Contours (broad to narrow, rule tailoring)

2. Case Illustration (introductory sentence, fact selection, reasoning and holding)

3. Nuts and Bolts (citations, quotations, past tense)

Examples: The sample memos in Chapter 8 contain examples of rule and explanation paragraphs (see pages 147–49, 154–55, 157–58).

Factual Background: Your client, Dr. Tanisha Greene, was the on-call cardiologist when a patient arrived in the emergency department suffering from symptoms of appendicitis. Dr. Greene refused to consult on the case and referred him to the proper specialty. The patient has sued her and several other physicians, based on an infection caused by a delay in the surgery. You plan to assert that no physician-patient relationship arose between Dr. Greene and the patient.

Exercise: Set out below are two charts. The first contains sentences that may belong in a rule statement about the creation of a physician-patient relationship. Which one doesn't belong? Why not? Please put them in a useful order for a rule statement. The second chart contains sentences for an explanation paragraph containing a case illustration. Which one does not belong? Why not? Please put them in a useful order for an explanation paragraph.

continued

RULE SENTENCES
(1) Affirmative acts toward treatment may include listening to symptoms, evaluating information, and contributing to the patient's treatment plan. *Id.*
(2) The physician in our case likely did not create a physician-patient relationship because she refused to see the patient and had no contract to treat him.
(3) No direct contact between the two is required, nor must the two deal directly with one another at all for the relationship to arise. *Id.* at 45.
(4) A physician-patient relationship can be based on a contract or on the physician's acts. *Tower v. Pythe*, 576 P.2d 43, 44 (Cal. 2017).
(5) Where a physician is on call and is consulted for advice, a physician-patient relationship arises where the on-call physician takes affirmative actions toward the patient's treatment. *Id.*

EXPLANATION SENTENCES
(1) The court held that a physician-patient relationship existed based on the cardiologist's listening to symptoms, his diagnosis of the condition, and his statement that no further treatment was needed. *Id.*
(2) Based on the cardiologist's diagnosis—gastric rather than cardiac problems—the emergency room physician allowed the patient to leave. *Id.*
(3) An on-call cardiologist created a physician-patient relationship with a patient, for example, when the cardiologist listened to a patient's symptoms, said the patient was likely suffering from gastric symptoms, and advised no further treatment. *Id.* at 46.
(4) A patient had presented in the emergency room with crushing chest pain. *Id.* The treating physician telephoned an on-call cardiologist and described the symptoms. *Id.*
(5) The patient was in fact suffering from a disabling heart attack. *Id.*
(6) The on-call physician says, "This patient has gastric problems, not cardiac problems. I think he should be allowed to leave the hospital now, without further treatment."

Exercise 25

 *Lightning Round*

Skills Tested (explained on pages 63–65):

1. Rule Contours (broad to narrow, rule tailoring)
2. Nuts and Bolts (citations, quotations)

Examples: The sample memos in Chapter 8 contain examples of rule and explanation paragraphs (see pages 147–49, 154–55, 157–58).

Legal Principles: These are provisions from the Americans with Disabilities Act (ADA):

1. "The term 'disability' means, with respect to an individual, a physical or mental impairment that substantially limits one or more major life activities of such individual." 42 U.S.C. § 12102(1)(A).

2. "An impairment that is episodic or in remission is a disability if it would substantially limit a major life activity when active." 42 U.S.C. § 12102(4)(D).

3. "The term 'qualified individual' means an individual who, with or without reasonable accommodation, can perform the essential functions of the employment position that such individual holds or desires." 42 U.S.C. § 12111(8).

4. "No covered entity shall discriminate against a qualified individual with a disability on the basis of disability in regard to job application procedures, the hiring, advancement, or discharge of employees, employment compensation, job training, or other terms, conditions, and privileges of employment." 42 U.S.C. § 12112(a).

Factual Background: Javier Fuentes alleges he was fired after his employer found out he suffers from migraine headaches. Mr. Fuentes has a migraine about once every month or two, lasting for several days and causing him to miss work. His supervisor was sad to see him go but said he needed a more dependable employee. Mr. Fuentes has sued under the ADA.

Legal Issue: Is Mr. Fuentes's condition, intermittent migraine headaches, a disability under the Americans with Disabilities Act?

Exercise: Identify five specific problems with the following rule and explanation paragraph:

> Under the Americans with Disabilities Act, "[t]he term 'qualified individual' means an individual who, with or without reasonable accommodation, can perform the essential functions of the employment position that such individual holds or desires." No covered entity shall discriminate against a qualified individual with a disability on the basis of disability in regard to job application procedures, the hiring, advancement, or discharge of employees, employment compensation, job training, or other terms, conditions, and privileges of employment. A disability is an impairment that substantially limits one or more major life activities of an individual. An episodic impairment is a disability "if it would substantially limit a major life activity when active."

Exercise 26

 *Lightning Round*

Skill Tested (**explained on page 64**):

Treatment Depth (parenthetical, short explanation)

Examples: The sample memos in Chapter 8 contain examples of rule and explanation paragraphs and parentheticals (see pages 147–49, 154–55, 157–58).

Exercise: Which of the following rule and explanation paragraphs is more effective? Why?

Option A

> A tavern keeper owes its patrons a duty to protect them from foreseeable injuries caused by other patrons. *Stevens v. Jefferson*, 436 So. 2d 33, 34 (Fla. 1983). A plaintiff can prove foreseeability by showing that a similar harm-causing incident happened before. *Id.* at 35. Courts have imposed a duty to protect against injury caused by another in many other comparable contexts. For example, a poodle owner was liable when her dog bit a jogger on a walk because the dog had bitten a child at the neighborhood dog park sixteen days earlier. *See Wells v. Hickman*, 698 So. 2d 921, 923 (Fla. 2001). Similarly, when their ten-year-old son broke an elderly neighbor's window with a large rock after being caught throwing rocks of various sizes several times before and they did not punish him, his parents were held liable. *Stanford v. Smith*, 522 So. 2d 533, 535 (Fla. 1996).

Option B

> A tavern keeper owes its patrons a duty to protect them from foreseeable injuries caused by other patrons. *Stevens v. Jefferson*, 436 So. 2d 33, 34 (Fla. 1983). A plaintiff can prove foreseeability by showing that a similar harm-causing incident happened before. *Id.* at 35. Courts have imposed a duty to protect against injury caused by another in many other comparable contexts. *See, e.g.*, *Wells v. Hickman*, 698 So. 2d 921, 923 (Fla. 2001) (holding a dog owner liable for injuries from dog bite when his dog had bitten before); *Stanford v. Smith*, 522 So. 2d 533, 535 (Fla. 1996) (concluding that parents were liable for damages from their child's rock throwing because he had thrown rocks earlier).

Exercise 27

 *Lightning Round*

Skills Tested (explained on pages 63–65):

1. Rule Contours (rule tailoring)
2. Case Illustration (introductory sentence, fact selection, reasoning and holding)
3. Nuts and Bolts (no client facts, past tense)

Examples: The sample memos in Chapter 8 contain examples of rule and explanation paragraphs (see pages 147–49, 154–55, 157–58).

Legal Principles:

1. To prove alienation of affection, the plaintiff must show (1) there was a marriage with love and affection, (2) the love and affection was alienated and destroyed, and (3) the defendant's wrongful and malicious acts caused the loss of love and affection.
2. To cause the loss of love and affection, a defendant need not be the initiator in the relationship but must only be a willing participant, making occasions for a relationship to develop.

Background Facts: David Moll sued Manuel Cortez for alienation of affection after his wife, Tonya Moll, and Mr. Cortez had an affair, leading to their divorce. Mrs. Moll met Mr. Cortez at work and was extremely attracted to him. She pursued a relationship with him for three months before Mr. Cortez relented, and then the two of them began a sexual affair in which Mr. Cortez fully and willingly participated. Mr. Cortez claims that he is an innocent party because Mrs. Moll seduced him and so it was not his fault that the marriage broke up.

Legal Issue: Can Mr. Moll prove that Mr. Cortez caused the loss of love and affection in his marriage?

Exercise: Below is a series of sentences that, together, will form a case illustration relevant to the issue of whether Mr. Cortez caused the loss of love and affection in the Molls' marriage. For each section, there are two choices. Which one in each set is best suited for a case illustration based on the facts and legal principles set out above? Why? What is wrong with the other ones?

I. Section One

A. In *Ward v. Beaton*, there was sufficient evidence to show the defendant caused the loss of love and affection. 539 S.E.2d 30, 33 (N.C. Ct. App. 2000).

B. The defendant need not lure the spouse away from the marriage to cause alienation of affection if the defendant willingly participated in the affair. *See Ward v. Beaton*, 539 S.E.2d 30, 33 (N.C. Ct. App. 2000).

II. Section Two

A. Patricia Ward sued Kristen Beaton for alienation of affection. *Id.* at 32. Ms. Beaton had an affair with Mr. Ward, just as Mr. Cortez had an affair with Mrs. Moll. *Id.* Mr. Ward was a captain at the Mitchell County Sheriff's department and responded to several domestic disturbance calls from Ms. Beaton's home. *Id.* at 33. She then began calling him at work and inviting him to her home. *Id.* Once, she came to the police station, smelling of alcohol. She refused to take a breathalyzer test and insisted Mr. Ward drive her home. *Id.*

B. In *Ward*, a wife sued her husband's mistress for alienation of affection after they had a sexual affair. *Id.* at 32. The husband, a police captain, met the defendant after he responded to a call at her home. *Id.* The defendant then continued to contact the husband at work, inviting him to her home and visiting him at the station. *Id.*

III. Section Three

A. Within a few months of their meeting, the defendant and the husband moved in together, and they began a sexual relationship. *Id.* Mrs. Ward said she and Mr. Ward used to have a "perfect marriage" and that Mr. Ward was a good husband and father. *Id.*

B. Within a few months of their meeting, the defendant and the husband moved in together, and they began a sexual relationship. *Id.*

IV. Section Four

A. The court held that the evidence was sufficient to prove the defendant was a cause of the alienation because her conduct showed she willingly participated in the affair, even if she did not intentionally act to lure the husband away from his wife. *Id.*

B. The court holds that the trial court did not err in denying the defendant's motion for directed verdict because the evidence is sufficient to show the defendant was a cause of the alienation; her conduct showed she, like Mr. Cortez, willingly participated in the affair, even if she did not intentionally act to lure the husband away from his wife. *Id.*

Exercise 28

 *Lightning Round*

Skill Tested (explained on pages 63–64):

Rule Contours (choice of authority, broad to narrow, rule tailoring)

Examples: The sample memos in Chapter 8 contain examples of rule and explanation paragraphs (see pages 147–49, 154–55, 157–58).

Factual Background: Anvi Padavala sued Mayra Karna for intentional infliction of emotional distress and invasion of privacy and seeks actual and punitive damages. The two women are former best friends and apartment roommates. Padavala had applied for her dream job working for a top accounting firm. The firm called their apartment to speak to Padavala about scheduling an interview, but Padavala was not at home. Karna took the call and promised to deliver the urgent message, but she never did. Though she knew that Padavala desperately wanted the job, Karna thought it was a bad idea. The accounting firm was known for its intense, high-stress environment, and Karna worried that working at such a place would harm Padavala's mental health. Out of her concern for her best friend's wellbeing, Karna didn't tell Padavala about the call. Padavala eventually learned about the missed interview opportunity, but by the time she found out, the job was filled.

Legal Issue: Does Karna's conduct support a claim for punitive damages based on malicious conduct?

Exercise: The chart below contains some rules relating to punitive damages. Decide which ones are needed for a rule and explanation paragraph relating to the above factual background and legal issue and which order the necessary items should be in. Explain your reasoning for each choice.

RULES
(1) Malice requires a specific intent to cause substantial injury or harm. Tex. Civ. Prac. & Rem. Code Ann. § 41.001(7).
(2) The elements of fraud are a material misrepresentation, which was false, and which was either known to be false when made or was asserted without knowledge of its truth, which was intended to be acted upon, which was relied upon, and which caused injury. *Sears, Roebuck & Co. v. Meadows*, 877 S.W.2d 281, 282 (Tex. 1994).

(3) Punitive damages are recoverable only when the harm results from fraud, malice, or gross negligence. Tex. Civ. Prac. & Rem. Code Ann. § 41.003(a).

(4) Malice must be proven by clear and convincing evidence. *Echostar Satellite L.L.C. v. Aguilar*, 394 S.W.3d 276, 292 (Tex. App. 2012).

(5) Malice must be proven by clear and convincing evidence. *Wilen v. Falkenstein*, 191 S.W.3d 791, 800 (Tex. App. 2006).

(6) A defendant is not liable for punitive damages if she acted in good faith and without wrongful intention. *Coinmach Corp. v. Aspenwood Apartment Corp.*, 417 S.W.3d 909, 922 (Tex. 2013).

(7) Specific intent means that the actor desires the consequences of her act or believes the consequences are substantially certain to result. *Seber v. Union Pac. R.R. Co.*, 350 S.W.3d 640, 654 (Tex. App. 2011).

(8) A defendant is not liable for punitive damages if she acted in good faith and without wrongful intention. *Wilen v. Falkenstein*, 191 S.W.3d 791, 800 (Tex. App. 2006).

Exercise 29

 *Deeper Dive*

....

Skills Tested (explained on pages 63–64):

1. Rule Contours (broad to narrow, rule tailoring)
2. Treatment Depth (parenthetical, short explanation, case illustration)

....

Examples: The sample memos in Chapter 8 contain examples of rule and explanation paragraphs and parentheticals (see pages 147–49, 154–55, 157–58).

Factual Background: You are assigned to prosecute Cameron Vu, who had a box cutter knife in his pants pocket when he robbed a convenience store. As the clerk opened the register to give Vu his change, Vu demanded money and gestured toward the knife. The knife remained in Vu's pocket but was partially visible during the robbery. Fearing the knife, the clerk complied.

Legal Principles: You are analyzing whether the knife can be deemed a "deadly weapon" when used as Vu did. You have found two cases addressing the deadly weapon issue; summaries of the cases are set out in the boxes below.

Billey v. State, 401 S.W.3d 417, 417 (Tenn. 2013).

A weapon can be considered a "deadly weapon" without the actual infliction of harm. Here, the assailant merely displayed a sharp, six-inch knife, but the knife was at a distance of two feet from the victim. The victim complied because of the threat received by the display of the weapon; she feared a serious bodily injury. As a consequence, the defendant left the store with three hundred dollars. We therefore hold that the knife's dangerousness, the victim's close proximity to the knife, the victim's evident fear of the knife, and the defendant's showing of the knife provide sufficient evidence to support the knife's designation as a deadly weapon.

Lucero v. State, 320 S.W.3d 612, 612 (Tenn. 2010).

To be a "deadly weapon," a weapon need not actually be used; it is sufficient if the weapon is displayed in a manner conveying an express or implied threat that serious bodily injury or death will be inflicted if the aggressor's desire is not satisfied. Here, Lucero was accused of aggravated robbery based on stealing a woman's purse outside a grocery store. The alleged deadly weapon was a long screwdriver. During the tussle over the purse, the screwdriver remained several feet from the victim, on the floor of the defendant's car. The victim could only see the tip of the screwdriver's handle. The victim was afraid the defendant would hit her, not that he would use the screwdriver. Based on these facts, the screwdriver was not a deadly weapon.

Exercise:

(1) Please draft a rule using these two cases.

(2) Now think about how to explain the law further, considering the facts of your case. Using just one of the cases, please set out your explanation of the law in whatever manner (parenthetical, short explanation, or full case illustration) you believe the reader would find most helpful.

Exercise 30

 *Deeper Dive*

....

Skills Tested (explained on pages 63–65):

1. Rule Contours (rule tailoring)
2. Treatment Depth (parenthetical, short explanation, case illustration)
3. Case Illustration (introductory sentence, fact selection, reasoning and holding)
4. Nuts and Bolts (citations, quotations, past tense)

....

Examples: The sample memos in Chapter 8 contain examples of rule and explanation paragraphs and parentheticals (see pages 147–49, 154–55, 157–58).

Factual Background: Mr. and Mrs. Blaine were worried about their twenty-year-old son, Andrew Blaine, because he had joined a religious group that they considered a cult. They thought the group was brainwashing him. They became particularly concerned after Andrew began saying that the world was doomed and he couldn't wait to meet the Supreme Leader in the afterlife, the sooner the better. The Blaines hired a group of men who said they could deprogram Andrew from the cult's influence. The deprogrammers abducted Andrew on a Friday afternoon around 2:00 p.m. They held him in a locked room with no access to a phone or computer over the weekend, trying various deprogramming techniques on him. Andrew did not cooperate. When it became clear that their efforts would not succeed, the deprogrammers decided to work with Andrew's parents to have him civilly committed on Tuesday. Andrew, however, was able to escape Monday night around midnight, so no civil commitment proceedings were ever initiated. Andrew's roommate had reported him missing to the police, and the police were looking for him all weekend, which the deprogrammers knew. Andrew sued the deprogrammers for false imprisonment, and they asserted the defense of necessity.

Legal Issue: Did the deprogrammers detain Andrew longer than allowed by the necessity defense to false imprisonment?

Legal Background: The following two cases provide the legal background for the necessity defense to false imprisonment:

Fortenberry v. Graham, 267 N.W.2d 643, 647 (Minn. 1979).

The defense of necessity has three elements. The first element is that the defendants must have acted under the reasonable belief that there was a danger of imminent physical injury to the plaintiff or others. Second, the confinement must last no longer than necessary to get the person to the proper lawful authorities. Third, the defendants must use the least restrictive means available to prevent the harm. No specific time period can be set as to the acceptable length of confinement, as it will vary with the circumstances of each case. The failure to even attempt to use any lawful alternatives will defeat a necessity defense.

In this case, the deprogrammers confined Fortenberry for five days, the first four of which were business days. During this time, they handcuffed Fortenberry to a bed, deprived him of all access to the outside world, and monitored him constantly. They made no effort to turn him over to the police or initiate civil commitment proceedings under Minnesota law. Fortenberry is free only because he escaped. Here, where the defendants held the plaintiff for five days, including four business days, and did not even try to resort to any lawful means available to them, they cannot establish the necessity defense to false imprisonment as a matter of law.

Patrick v. Owens, 398 N.W.2d 21, 28 (Minn. 1999).

The second element of the necessity defense is that the defendant confined the plaintiff no longer than necessary to get the plaintiff to the lawful authorities. A defendant who deliberately conceals the plaintiff's location from the police cannot establish that the detention should have continued. Patrick moved for summary judgment, arguing that the evidence conclusively established that Owens held him too long, especially in the face of a police search.

Owens abducted Patrick on his parents' request to attempt to deprogram him from the influences of the Harmony Initiative. Owens took him on Tuesday at 3:00 p.m. and heard later that evening, around 9:20 p.m., that a police hunt was underway for Patrick after his employer reported to the police that he had not

continued

shown up for work. Owens got scared and decided to release Patrick, which he did on Tuesday at 11:30 p.m. Given that Owens detained Patrick for under nine hours and released him shortly after learning of the police search for him, we conclude that a fact issue exists as to the reasonability of the length of detention, and thus Patrick is not entitled to summary judgment on the second element of Owens's necessity defense.

Exercise: To demonstrate different ways to use the same authorities, complete the following tasks:

A. Parenthetical: Write a synthesized subrule for the second element, using *Fortenberry*'s language about attempts to use lawful alternatives and *Patrick*'s language about concealment from the police. State the synthesized subrule in one sentence, cite both cases, and include parentheticals for both case citations.

B. Short explanation: Write a one- to two-sentence explanation, with citations, for each case. These explanations should serve as a miniature case illustration for the following subrule: The acceptable length of confinement is not absolute but will vary with each case.

C. Case illustration: Write a complete case illustration of the *Fortenberry* case to illustrate this subrule of the second element: The failure to even attempt to use any lawful alternatives will defeat a necessity defense.

Exercise 31

 *Deeper Dive*

Skills Tested (explained on pages 64–65):

1. Case Illustration (introductory sentence, fact selection, reasoning and holding)
2. Multiple Case Illustrations
3. Nuts and Bolts (citations, past tense)

Examples: The sample memos in Chapter 8 contain examples of rule and explanation paragraphs (see pages 147–49, 154–55, 157–58).

Factual Background: You represent Timothy Wagner, who is charged with robbing a store. Six hours after the robbery, the store clerk spoke to a detective. The clerk said in a recorded statement that Wagner threatened violence if she called the police. The clerk described the events with a shaky voice. The detective recorded the statement at the store, where she had continued to work to the end of her shift.

Legal Principles: The clerk is now unavailable to testify, but the prosecutor would like to use the recording at trial. Normally, an out-of-court statement would be excluded from testimony under the hearsay rule, but an exception might apply here. The prosecutor hopes that the recording will fall under the "excited utterance" exception, which allows statements to be admitted at trial if they are made soon after an upsetting event and under the mental stress of that event. The *Hamsfield* case explains this law:

> *Hamsfield v. State*, 55 S.W.3d 333, 338 (Ky. 2012).
>
> The issue is whether the trial court correctly admitted at trial an audiotape describing an alleged assault by Coach Bob Smith; we hold that the tape should not have been admitted at trial. Detective Johnson made the recording during an interview with a teacher, Sandy Wells, five hours after Smith allegedly slapped Wells during a high school basketball game at the school where the two worked.
>
> The trial court admitted a portion of Wells's recorded statement under the excited utterance exception to the hearsay rule. Hearsay is an out-of-court statement that is offered to prove the truth of the matter asserted. Hearsay is generally inadmissible.

continued

> We conclude that the statement was not an excited utterance. As she spoke, Wells was clearly upset. But, she responded calmly to questions. There was no indication that she was responding out of emotion or spontaneously. And, five hours had passed since the event. The hallmark of the excited utterance is that the declarant be dominated by the emotion of the event—that hallmark is missing here.

Exercise: You have already set out your conclusion, rule, and first case illustration in your draft memo below. Now, add a second case illustration, using *Hamsfield*, connecting it to the first and including the required parts of the case illustration.

Your Draft Memo

It is a close case as to whether the clerk's statement after the robbery was properly admitted under the excited utterance exception to the hearsay rule.

Statements other than those made by a declarant testifying at trial are generally not admissible at trial. *Zuliani v. State*, 27 S.W.3d 345, 349 (Ky. 2015). Such statements are considered hearsay and are only admissible if they fit within an exception to the hearsay rule, such as the "excited utterance" exception. *Id.* "Excited utterances" are those statements relating to a stressful or otherwise exciting situation, such that the statement is made without reflection and is thus considered more reliable. *Id.* To determine whether a statement is an excited utterance, courts can consider the time elapsed between the event and the statement, but the touchstone of this hearsay exception is whether the declarant is still emotionally excited by the event. *Id.* at 350.

A statement was considered an excited utterance where twenty hours had passed between an assault and the subsequent statement because the declarant was still afraid of the assailant and had not separated from him during the twenty hours. *Id.* at 351. In *Zuliani*, a domestic assault victim spoke with the police about twenty hours after the assault. *Id.* The victim's statements were excited utterances because her demeanor and tone of voice indicated that she was still under the stress of the assault when she spoke. *Id.* It is this stress, the court emphasized, that is the most important consideration for the excited utterance analysis. *Id.*

[Second case illustration using *Hamsfield* will go here.]

In the case at hand, the statement may or may not be considered an excited utterance . . . [Application would continue here.]

Exercise 32

 *Deeper Dive*

Skills Tested (explained on pages 63–65):

1. Rule Contours (broad to narrow, rule tailoring)
2. Case Illustration (introductory sentence, fact selection)
3. Nuts and Bolts (citations, no client facts, quotations, past tense)

Examples: The sample memos in Chapter 8 contain examples of rule and explanation paragraphs (see pages 147–49, 154–55, 157–58).

Background Facts: Andrew Calhoon and his friend, Mike Potter, went out drinking to celebrate Calhoon's being offered his dream job earlier that day. At the end of the celebration, Calhoon was not feeling well. He gave Potter his phone password so Potter could call them an Uber. Unbeknownst to Calhoon, Potter used Calhoon's password again during the ride home to open Calhoon's Twitter app. As a joke, Potter impersonated Calhoon and posted an offensive Tweet. Calhoon's prospective employer saw the offensive Tweet and rescinded the job offer. Calhoon sued Potter for invasion of privacy, arguing that he gave Calhoon his password for a particular purpose and that Calhoon went beyond the scope of his permission. Potter has argued that Calhoon giving him his password meant Calhoon no longer had any reasonable expectation of privacy in his phone and that he thus had Calhoon's implied permission to access his phone for any reason.

Legal Issue: Is a court likely to find that Mr. Potter invaded Mr. Calhoon's privacy by intentionally intruding into his private affairs, namely his Twitter account?

Exercise: Based on these background facts and legal issue, revise this rule and explanation paragraph and accompanying case illustration to make them more effective. Explain the reasoning for your changes.

continued

When assessing whether an invasion is offensive, courts require the intrusion to be "unjustified or unwarranted." *Vaughn v. Drennon*, 202 S.W.3d 308, 320 (Tex. App. 2006). There can be no intrusion on seclusion if the plaintiff consented to the defendant's conduct. *Farrington v. Sysco Food Servs.*, 865 S.W.2d 247, 253 (Tex. App. 1993). Invasion of privacy based on intrusion on seclusion has two elements: (1) an intentional intrusion on another's solitude, seclusion, or private affairs or concerns, which (2) would be highly offensive to a reasonable person. *Valenzuela v. Aquino*, 853 S.W.2d 512, 513 (Tex. 1993).

Exceeding the scope of a person's consent can constitute an invasion of privacy. *See Oberman v. Gateway, Inc.*, 900 S.W.2d 160, 172-73 (Tex. App. 1996). In *Oberman*, Yelp developed a Friend Finder feature that allowed Yelp users to locate other Yelp users by comparing email addresses of registered Yelp users to email addresses in the user's contacts app. *Id.* at 168. This feature was available only to registered Yelp users, who had to agree to Yelp's terms of service and privacy policy. Yelp users brought a class action lawsuit against Yelp after they found out that Yelp had uploaded all of their contacts. They argued they had agreed to let Yelp access their contacts but not to upload them. That is similar to our case because Mr. Calhoon says he only authorized Mr. Potter to call an Uber, not to send a Tweet. Yelp moved for summary judgment, which the court denied. *Id.* at 173. The court stated that "consent is only effective if the person alleging harm consented to the particular conduct or to substantially the same conduct, and if the alleged tortfeasor did not exceed the scope of that consent" because "consent is not absolute, but rather a matter of degree." *Id.* at 172-73, 176. Based on the language of Yelp's policies and procedures, the court concludes there is a fact issue as to whether Yelp acted within the scope of the users' consent or exceeded it by uploading their contacts rather than only accessing them. *Id.* at 173.

Application

Summary of Skills Tested

In the application section, the legal writer weaves together the applicable law and the client's facts to yield a correct answer to the question posed. This portion of the memo, known as the affirmative argument, is at the core of the legal writer's task, containing the writer's reasoning process in a step-by-step sequence. A person without any particular background in the subject should be able to follow each step and see the conclusion's supporting logic. While earlier memo sections preview the important points and state the conclusion, this section is the only one that delves into the particular facts and reasoning and shows why they work together as they do.

To draft a useful application section, the writer must first be well acquainted with both the applicable law and the client's specific facts. The next step is to assemble and craft the separate arguments that support the correct answer to the client's question. Each argument should be supported by law and facts, but the degree of support will depend on the client's issue and the applicable law. To answer a highly fact-intensive question, the writer will probably have drafted a fact-intensive explanation section. This, in turn, will lead to an application that compares a number of specific client facts to facts from the applicable law. A writer would respond to a more straight-forward and less fact-intensive issue with fewer facts or perhaps a direct application of law to the client's facts, without extensive discussion of precedent.

SKILLS TESTED IN THIS CHAPTER	
SKILL	EXERCISE
Structure	36, 37, 38, 39, 40, 42, 43, 44
Effective Analogies	33, 34, 35, 38, 41, 43, 44
Show Your Work	35, 37, 38, 39, 40, 41, 42, 43, 44
Nuts and Bolts	35, 38, 39, 40, 42, 43, 44

These features of the application are described below, with additional guidance and variations.

Structure. A helpful affirmative argument begins with a thoughtfully constructed framework. To outline the framework, the writer can start with an overall thesis statement telling the reader how the entire application turns out. Be sure to begin the thesis statement with a clear shift, so the reader knows that the explanation is now giving way to something quite different. You can use words such as "Here" or "In the case at hand" to make this shift. Then, the outline continues with topic sentences that set out each distinct argument supporting the overall thesis. So that the reader can follow easily, the thesis and framework should track the same order and should feature the same key points as the rule and explanation.

An effective application should be structured around arguments as opposed to individual cases. Several cases may be required to make an effective affirmative argument, and those cases should be integrated to make a coherent argument. Regurgitating several cases in a row does not make an effective application. Similarly, arguments should be based on the language of the applicable legal rules, and when the application is based on a case illustration, the analysis should parallel the case illustration's structure.

Effective Analogies. To make the arguments that support the overall thesis, the writer must first decide whether to use a straight application of the rule or analogical reasoning. The decision will depend on the rule's complexity, the client's facts, and the applicable precedent. If, for example, the writer can answer the question simply by reference to the rule's terms, then analogies are not needed. A more complex or uncertain rule may call for the greater nuance that analogical reasoning can provide.

If the writer chooses to use analogical reasoning, the writer must first understand how to make appropriate comparisons. The analogies between precedent facts and client facts must be the most illuminating comparisons possible. Such comparisons should first be relevant, meaning that they matter to the rule. They should be presented so that the reader can clearly see the point, either by placing the two facts near one another or by using a pattern such that the comparison becomes evident. The writer should select precedent facts from those in the explanation—precedent facts should not pop up for the first time in the application, as this would be jarring to the reader's established understanding of the law.

Show Your Work. Once the writer selects the structure and arguments, the next step is to show each step of the reasoning as the argument develops. To do this, the writer should progress through the arguments, weaving precedent and current facts or reasoning together, working toward a conclusion. Each argument and step of analysis must be specific, leaving no guesswork for the reader. Near the end of each argument, the writer should reference the rule language that the argument satisfies, so the reader can see exactly how the analysis matters to the rule and in turn leads to the conclusion. Once an argument is complete, the writer should transition explicitly to the next argument, so the reader knows that more argument is to come.

Nuts and Bolts. To keep the reader's focus on the client's case and help ensure clarity, consider discussing client facts before the precedent case facts when weaving them together. In the application, a citation need not follow every sentence. Where the writer references a rule or a specific aspect of a precedent case, however, a citation ensures the reader sees where that information comes from.

Throughout the application, maintain an objective tone. As with the rest of the memo, the goal here is the correct answer, no matter whether that helps or hurts the client.

You can try your hand at these skills in the exercises that follow; annotated sample answers are set out in the back of this volume for the even-numbered problems. The sample memos in Chapter 8 demonstrate how to write effective application sections.

Exercise 33

(15) *Lightning Round*

Skill Tested (**explained on page 92**):

Effective Analogies (how to analogize, relevant comparisons)

Examples: The sample memos in Chapter 8 contain examples of application sections (see pages 149, 155–56, 158–59).

Exercise: Answer the following questions, which test your ability to make effective analogies and relevant comparisons. Please explain the basis for the answer you choose and why you didn't choose the others.

a. Which is the closest comparison? The sun is to the moon as:

   i.   a flashlight is to a light bulb

   ii. a hot dog is to a cherry

   iii. a basketball is to an orange

b. Which is the closest comparison? A curtain is to a window as:

   i.   sheets are to a mattress

   ii. sunglasses are to eyes

   iii. a switch is to a lamp

c. Consider a group containing a bike, a doll, a scooter, and a pickup truck.

   i.   If the doll is excluded from the group, what is the relevant common factor among the remaining items?

   ii. If the pickup truck is excluded from the group, what is the relevant common factor among the remaining items?

d. Which is a correct logical argument?

   i.   All birds lay eggs. A penguin lays eggs. Therefore, a penguin is a bird.

   ii. All birds lay eggs. A penguin is a bird. Therefore, a penguin lays eggs.

Exercise 34

🕑 *Lightning Round*

Skill Tested (explained on page 92):

Effective Analogies (how to analogize, relevant comparisons)

Examples: The sample memos in Chapter 8 contain examples of application sections (see pages 149, 155–56, 158–59).

Factual Background: Two men went hunting in the woods one morning. An hour into their trip, one of the men died from a gunshot wound after the rifle his friend was carrying accidentally fired. The safety was engaged, but the gun nevertheless fired after the man carrying it tripped and banged it into a tree. The deceased's estate sued the gun manufacturer, alleging a design defect relating to the gun's trigger mechanism, which was designed by Andrew Baker. An expert who examined the gun found a small amount of soft dirt in the Baker trigger mechanism, which caused it to misalign and prevent the safety from properly engaging, so that when the gun banged into the tree, the gun discharged. The theory of the case is that the design of that particular rifle model is defective because a small bit of debris in the rifle's Baker trigger mechanism should not cause it to malfunction and negate the safety.

Exercise: Assume you are researching the law on the plaintiff's design defect claim, and you find a case that is factually on point to the present case in all relevant respects except for the one fact identified in each chart entry below. Determine whether that factual difference between the plaintiff's case and the precedent case is legally significant. Would that factual difference make the case you found unusable in your analysis? Explain why or why not for each.

FACT	DIFFERENCE LEGALLY SIGNIFICANT?	WHY OR WHY NOT?
Plaintiff's case: hunting in the woods Precedent case: hunting in a field		
Plaintiff's case: small amount of soft dirt found in trigger mechanism Precedent case: small amount of soft grass found in trigger mechanism		

table continued

FACT	DIFFERENCE LEGALLY SIGNIFICANT?	WHY OR WHY NOT?
Plaintiff's case: gun was a rifle Precedent case: gun was a pistol		
Plaintiff's case: gun owner shot a friend Precedent case: gun owner shot himself		
Plaintiff's case: hunting in the day Precedent case: hunting at night		
Plaintiff's case: gun fired because debris prevented safety from working properly Precedent case: gun fired because safety was not turned on		
Plaintiff's case: rifle had a Baker trigger mechanism Precedent case: rifle had a different trigger mechanism (not Baker)		
Plaintiff's case: gun banged into a tree Precedent case: gun banged into a rock		

Exercise 35

 *Lightning Round*

Skills Tested (explained on pages 92–93):

1. Effective Analogies (relevant comparisons, proximity or pattern)
2. Show Your Work (be specific)
3. Nuts and Bolts (objective tone)

Examples: The sample memos in Chapter 8 contain examples of application sections (see pages 149, 155–56, 158–59).

Background Facts: Lara Marianne adopted a Labrador mix dog named Sadie at an animal shelter. Sadie's previous owners had surrendered her to the shelter because she snapped at their toddler. The toddler had grabbed Sadie's fur and would not let go, so Sadie responded by snapping the air near the child. Sadie did not make any contact with the toddler's skin, though she easily could have, and there was no injury. Sadie had never done anything else that could be considered aggressive or dangerous. The shelter personnel disclosed this information during the adoption process. Marianne keeps Sadie in an outdoor kennel and tethers the dog when Marianne is outside gardening. Two years after Marianne adopted Sadie, Marianne was jogging in the park with Sadie when another, faster jogger overtook the duo at very close range. Sadie was startled and grabbed the passer-by with her teeth, causing a small cut.

Legal Background: The key case on point is *Slack v. Khan*, which is summarized below:

> Sara and Will Khan owned Gideon, a German Shepherd dog that served as a service dog for Jon, their young son with autism. Gideon was a well-behaved dog that had never rushed at or bitten anyone. Gideon was so well trained that he hardly acknowledged others as he accompanied Jon throughout his day. When Jon played in the front yard, the Khans kept Gideon on a loose tether so he would not walk into the nearby busy street. One evening, Jon and Gideon were walking in the neighborhood when Gideon rushed at a passer-by, Lara Slack. Slack recoiled and fell, suffering a gash on her leg. Slack sued the Khans for her damages, based on

continued

> a strict liability theory. The Khans prevailed on summary judgment because the Khans had no reason to know that Gideon was dangerous. The court noted that the owner's knowledge turns on a dog's past actions, and only when the past actions are substantially similar to the one now at issue. The owner's knowledge is not based on the dog's breed or the manner in which it is housed or tethered.

Legal Issue: Could Marianne be strictly liable for the injury?

Exercise: A new associate is planning her memo addressing the strict liability issue, and she will be relying on *Slack*. She knows that she needs to use specific, substantive analogies to construct her application section. Of the following comparisons, which ones should she include? What is wrong with the others?

(1)   Like the owners in *Slack*, the owner here had no reason to know her dog would bite a person.

(2)   Like the owners in *Slack*, who had no indication that their dog would rush at a person, the owner here had no reason to know her dog would actually bite a person.

(3)   Based on *Slack*, the dog's tethering should not equate to knowledge on Marianne's part that her dog was extremely vicious and capable of mauling a person.

(4)   The court in *Slack* noted that the details of a dog's tethering should not equate to knowledge of dangerousness, so the tethering here should not equate to knowledge of dangerousness on Marianne's part.

(5)   Unlike the German Shepherd in *Slack*, Sadie is a Labrador, a breed known for its mild nature. Sadie is thus particularly unlikely to be a known dangerous dog.

(6)   Like *Slack*, the owners here could not have known that their dog would attack a person.

Exercise 36

 *Lightning Round*

....

Skill Tested (explained on page 92):

Structure (thesis statement, arguments rather than cases)

....

Examples: The sample memos in Chapter 8 contain examples of application sections (see pages 149, 155–56, 158–59).

Background Facts: Sam has owned Skipper the pit bull for four years. Skipper came from a rescue organization; he had been found as a stray. The person who brought Skipper to the shelter said he was "a bit difficult." There were no other behavior notes on file. In the four years that Sam has owned Skipper, Skipper has not bitten any people. Skipper has, however, mauled a cat and eaten four pigeons. Sam called you in a panic, stating that Skipper got out of the yard and bit a child on the arm. The child's parents are threatening to sue.

Legal Issue: Will Sam be strictly liable for the child's injury?

Exercise: The conclusion, rule, and explanation for a memo on this issue are set out below. Below those sections are three different examples of a thesis statement and topic sentences. Which one in each group is best suited to an application section based on the facts set out above and the law below? What is wrong with the other ones?

> Sam will not be strictly liable for the child's bite injuries because he had no reason to anticipate that his dog would bite a person.
>
> An animal's owner can be held strictly liable for injuries the animal causes if the owner had notice that the animal would cause that kind of harm. *Black v. Vinson*, 178 A.3d 1125, 1127 (Md. Ct. Spec. App. 2018). The owner must be on notice that the animal would cause the same kind of harm that is later at issue—the "particular mischief" that the owner had a basis to anticipate. *Id.* An animal's aggression toward other animals does not forecast aggression toward humans. *Id.* And, an animal's breed does not predict viciousness. *Id.*

continued

> A dog's owners were not strictly liable, for example, when their dog rushed at a passer-by and caused a fall but they had no prior indication that the dog would behave that way. *Id.* The dog in question was a Doberman that had previously barked at other dogs; the court noted, however, that neither an animal's breed nor its behavior toward other animals is an indication of future dangerousness toward humans. *Id.* The only hint that the owners knew the dog might behave that way was one owner's disputed statement that she could not control the dog. *Id.* This, the court found, did not amount to an iota of sufficient evidence, and the owners were not strictly liable. *Id.*

I. *Thesis Statement*

    A.   Here, Sam will probably not be strictly liable because he had no specific indication that Skipper would bite a person.

    B.   Here, the case of *Black v. Vinson* is helpful in resolving this issue.

    C.   Here, Sam will probably not be strictly liable.

II. *First Topic Sentence*

    A.   Sam did not know that his dog was aggressive.

    B.   Sam knew Skipper was a "bit difficult."

    C.   Sam had no specific sign that Skipper would bite, but only the vague piece of information that Skipper was a "bit difficult."

III. *Second Topic Sentence*

    A.   Neither the fact that Skipper is a pit bull nor his aggressiveness toward other animals predicts aggressiveness toward humans.

    B.   Neither a dog's breed nor its aggressiveness toward other animals indicates future dangerousness toward humans.

    C.   In the *Black* case, neither the dog's breed nor its aggressiveness toward other animals was considered a prediction of future dangerousness.

Exercise 37

 **Lightning Round**

Skills Tested (explained on pages 92–93):

1. Structure (thesis statement, analysis parallels case illustration)
2. Show Your Work (weave client facts and case information, tie back to the rule)

Examples: The sample memos in Chapter 8 contain examples of application sections (see pages 149, 155–56, 158–59).

Background Facts: You represent Michael Wagner, who robbed a store while pointing to a stiletto knife; its handle protruded slightly from his pocket throughout the robbery. At the time he reached over to the cash register and grabbed $700 in cash, Wagner pushed a clerk out of the way, pointed to his knife, and said, "I'm going to filet you right now if you try to stop me." He did not open or brandish the knife. The clerk looked at the knife and backed away as Wagner left with the money.

Legal Issue: Is the stiletto knife, when so used, a "deadly weapon"?

Legal Principles: The conclusion, rule, and explanation for a memo based on these facts and this issue are set out below:

> Wagner's stiletto knife will probably be considered a deadly weapon because Wagner showed the weapon and made a threat, and the clerk retreated in response.
>
> If a weapon, as used, is capable of causing death or serious bodily injury, it is a deadly weapon. *Billey v. State*, 333 S.W.3d 34, 36 (Tex. 2017). To make this determination, courts will consider expert testimony regarding the potential deadliness of the weapon as well as the surrounding circumstances. *Id.* The surrounding circumstances include any verbal threats, any brandishing of the weapon, the distance between defendant and victim, the victim's fear of serious injury, any witness descriptions of the weapon, and the defendant's intent to use the weapon to inflict serious injury. *Id.*

continued

A weapon was considered a deadly weapon where the defendant made an implied threat and showed a partially unsheathed hunting knife during a robbery. *Id.* In that case, the defendant was robbing a store when the victim asked if he was "kidding" about the robbery. *Id.* at 37. In response, the defendant displayed the weapon and said he "wasn't kidding," although he never used the knife or injured the victim in any way. *Id.*

Even without an express threat, the knife's partial exposure and statement that the defendant "wasn't kidding" presented an implied threat of injury. *Id.* at 35. Whether or not the defendant actually intended to carry out the threat, the threat had its desired effect, in that the victim handed over the money. *Id.* In addition, the defendant was close enough to the victim to carry out the threat. *Id.* The knife was therefore considered a deadly weapon. *Id.* at 40.

Exercise: The application section following this conclusion, rule, and explanation could be written in six parts, which are set out in the table below. The table also includes a part that does not belong in the application section. Which part does not belong? What is the right order for the other parts? Please explain your reasoning.

PARTS OF THE APPLICATION SECTION
(1) The partially exposed knife together with a verbal threat probably mean that the knife amounts to a deadly weapon, just as the partial display of a knife and threat were the basis of a deadly weapon finding in *Billey*. *Id.*
(2) By pointing to the knife while making a verbal threat, Wagner implied that he would harm the clerk with the knife. Wagner's threat—to "filet" the clerk—was more explicit than the threat in *Billey*, where the defendant partially exposed a knife and stated that he "wasn't kidding" about the robbery. *Id.* Because the threat and weapon in *Billey* supported a deadly weapon finding, the threat and weapon probably will here as well.
(3) Thus, because the knife, threat, and clerk's reaction in the case at hand are equivalent to or more threatening than those in *Billey*, the knife here is probably a deadly weapon.
(4) Here, Wagner's stiletto knife will probably be considered a deadly weapon because Wagner pointed to the knife, he made a verbal threat, and the clerk responded in fear.

(5) In *Windsor*, a weapon was not a deadly weapon when the victim did not see the weapon and the victim's compliance was based on the defendant's words, not the weapon. *State v. Windsor*, 23 S.W.3d 33, 45 (Tex. 2011).

(6) The clerk here retreated in response to the threat, just as the clerk in *Billey* complied and turned over cash to the defendant. *Id.* The clerk's reaction in *Billey* confirmed that the weapon and threat supported a deadly weapon finding, *id.*, and the same is true here.

(7) Moreover, the clerk's retreat in reaction to Wagner's threat is further evidence that the weapon is properly considered a deadly weapon.

Exercise 38

 *Lightning Round*

Skills Tested (explained on pages 92–93):

1. Structure (analysis parallels case illustration)
2. Effective Analogies (proximity or pattern)
3. Show Your Work (weave client facts and case information)
4. Nuts and Bolt (citation)

Examples: The sample memos in Chapter 8 contain examples of application sections (see pages 149, 155–56, 158–59).

Background Facts: Francis Glory is a professional fountain builder. After a particularly difficult installation, a customer publicly accused Glory of stealing part of the installation, namely a large statue. That accusation proved to be baseless, and Glory sued the customer for defamation. The customer asserted in defense that Glory is a general or limited purpose public figure. The customer based this assertion on Glory's participation in a fountain-builders' business association and his service on the school board.

Legal Issue: Can Francis Glory be considered a general or limited purpose public figure?

Legal Principles: The conclusion, rule, and explanation for a memo based on these facts and this issue are set out below:

> Francis Glory is neither a limited purpose nor general purpose public figure. There are two categories of public figures: (1) general purpose public figures and (2) limited purpose public figures. *Pickens v. Cordia*, 433 S.W.3d 179, 185 (Tex. App. 2014). General purpose public figures are people with household names, who have achieved pervasive notoriety and are thus public figures for all purposes. *Id.* Limited purpose public figures are people who are public figures just for a particular issue or controversy. *Id.*
>
> Energy executive T. Boone Pickens was neither a general nor limited purpose public figure in a defamation claim based on his son's personal blog. *Id.* The blog described the son's childhood and substance abuse. *Id.* at 179. Pickens sued his son for defamation; the son

> countered that the speech was protected because his father was a public figure based on being repeatedly interviewed and writing several articles for national business publications. *Id.*
>
> The articles and interviews were insufficient to establish either general purpose or limited purpose public figure status. *Id.* Pickens was not a general purpose public figure—he was well known in the energy business but was not more broadly famous. *Id.* At most, the court found, Pickens was a limited purpose public figure in the energy business. *Id.* In the energy business, Pickens had embraced publicity. *Id.* at 187. He had given interviews and written articles for a national business audience. *Id.* Still, Pickens's limited fame was unrelated to the statements in his lawsuit. *Id.* Pickens's limited fame in the energy business did not protect his son's statements about the family's home life. *Id.*

Exercise: A new associate has now drafted the application section and has asked you how he can improve it. He is particularly uncertain about the comparisons to precedent. What went wrong, and how can he fix it?

> Here, Glory participated in business and public life without reaching general or limited public figure status. Glory's local political and business activities are insufficient to make him a general purpose public figure. Glory was a school board member and a member of a business association concerning fountain-building and installation. He was well known but only in limited business circles. This is insufficient notoriety to be a general purpose public figure, as Glory's name was far from a household name. This is similar to Pickens.
>
> Even as to limited purpose public figure status, Glory's facts present a weak case. There is no evidence of Glory penning articles for national publications or seeking the spotlight. Glory did serve as a school board member, but even if that or his professional activities rendered him a limited purpose public figure, such status is only relevant if the particular issue that the person thrust himself into is the same one as in the lawsuit. That is not the case here, as the lawsuit is based on a stolen statue, while any limited purpose public figure status would be related to the fountain industry or the school board. This is an even weaker case than that of Pickens, who wrote articles for national business publications and gave interviews.
>
> Glory is therefore not a public figure for purposes of this lawsuit.

Exercise 39

 *Lightning Round*

Skills Tested (**explained on pages 92–93**):

1. Structure (base arguments on rules)
2. Show Your Work (be specific, tie back to the rule)
3. Nuts and Bolts (citation)

Examples: The sample memos in Chapter 8 contain examples of application sections (see pages 149, 155–56, 158–59).

Factual Background: Jason Friedman recently lost his job and became homeless, but he still owns his car. Until he gets back on his feet, he has been sleeping in his car. Inside, he has a pillow and blanket that he uses for sleeping, as well as food, water, and a flashlight, along with some clothing and toiletries. One night while Jason was sleeping, Paul Tomberg broke into Jason's car, intending to steal it, and sat down in the driver's seat. Paul ran off once he saw Jason stretched out in the back seat, but fortunately for Jason, a police officer was nearby and was able to quickly apprehend Paul.

Legal Background: Paul was charged with burglary. Under the laws of the state, a person commits burglary "if, without the effective consent of the owner, the person enters a habitation with intent to commit a felony, theft, or assault." Penal Code § 10.02(a)(1). A habitation is "a structure or vehicle adopted for the overnight accommodation of persons." *Id.* § 10.02(b)(3).

Legal Issue: Does Jason's vehicle constitute a habitation under the burglary statute?

Exercise: The following application paragraph has some shortcomings. Please explain what they are. Then rewrite the paragraph to structure it based on the rule and apply that rule to specific client facts. Your paragraph should be a complete unit of legal analysis, including opening and closing conclusions, rules, and legal analysis.

> A burglary is when someone breaks into a habitation. Jason slept overnight in his car, so it is obviously a habitation. Therefore, Paul committed a burglary when he broke into Jason's car, and he should be prosecuted.

Exercise 40

(15) Lightning Round

....

Skill Tested (explained on pages 92–93):

1. Structure (base arguments on rules)
2. Show Your Work (be specific, tie back to the rule)
3. Nuts and Bolts (objective tone)

....

Examples: The sample memos in Chapter 8 contain examples of application sections (see pages 149, 155–56, 158–59).

Legal Background: A dog owner is liable for injuries caused by her dog biting a person if the owner has notice of the dog's dangerous propensities and does not take reasonable measures to protect others from the danger the dog poses. *Forest v. Parker*, 598 S.W.2d 921, 923 (Mo. 1982). An owner is deemed to have notice of a dog's dangerous propensities if the dog has bitten someone before. *Id.* Certain dog breeds may be considered inherently dangerous. *Id.* Reasonable measures to protect others may include restraining and muzzling the dog, depending on the circumstances. *Id.*

Exercise: Ms. Cline sued Mr. Owens after his pit bull bit her. Which of the following sentences could be included in an effective rule-based analysis about his potential liability based solely on the rules set forth above? Explain your answer.

APPLICATION	APPROPRIATE?	WHY OR WHY NOT?
(1) Mr. Owens had notice that his dog was dangerous because his dog chewed through a fence last year.		
(2) Mr. Owens knew his dog was dangerous because his dog bit a child at the dog park in May.		
(3) Mr. Owens had to know his dog was dangerous because it bit Ms. Cline five times and only a vicious dog would do that.		

table continued

APPLICATION	APPROPRIATE?	WHY OR WHY NOT?
(4) Mr. Owens knew his pit bull was inherently dangerous.		
(5) Mr. Owens took reasonable measures to protect Ms. Cline from his dog by locking the dog in another room; the dog bit Ms. Cline only after she insisted on opening the door to the room.		
(6) Mr. Owens kept his dog behind a locked fence and posted a "Beware of Dog" sign, just like the defendant in *Forest*.		

Exercise 41

 *Deeper Dive*

....

Skills Tested (explained on pages 92–93):

1. Effective Analogies (relevant comparisons, proximity or pattern)

2. Show Your Work (weave client facts and case information)

....

Examples: The sample memos in Chapter 8 contain examples of application sections (see pages 149, 155–56, 158–59).

Background Facts: You represent Dr. Marco Antonio, who was the on-call cardiologist on the night that Marina Navarro came into the emergency room (ER) with severe pain in her abdomen and shortness of breath. The attending ER physician examined Navarro and called Dr. Antonio for a cardiac consultation. After hearing the symptoms, Dr. Antonio responded as follows: "This sounds gastrointestinal, not something I'm handling. Evaluate her a bit longer, and that's it. I'm done here. You should call the gastrointestinal specialist." The attending ER physician watched the patient for an hour and called Dr. Antonio again. Dr. Antonio answered, "I'm done here. I'm not doing this. This is outside my area completely." The attending physician did not call anyone else but discharged Navarro later that day. Navarro suffered a severe heart attack that evening.

Legal Issue: Did a physician-patient relationship arise between Dr. Antonio and Marina Navarro?

Exercise: The conclusion, rule, and explanation are set out below, followed by an application section and conclusion. The application section is underlined. The author knows that the application section is not sufficient but is not sure how to fix it. What is missing? Please write some suggested language for the author to add to the application section.

> A physician-patient relationship probably does not exist between Dr. Antonio and Maria Navarro because Dr. Antonio only listened to symptoms and suggested that Navarro see another physician.
>
> A physician-patient relationship is required for a medical malpractice claim; the relationship can be inferred from the acts and conduct of the parties. *Lection v. Dyll*, 65 S.W.3d 696, 704 (Tex. App. 2001).

continued

An on-call physician without a prior relationship to the patient may assume a duty if the physician takes some affirmative action such as evaluating the information provided and making a medical decision toward treating the patient. *Id.* A referral to another physician does not, without more, create a physician-patient relationship. *Id.* at 708.

An on-call neurologist created a physician-patient relationship, for example, when he diagnosed a patient, stated no other treatment was necessary, and concurred with the patient's discharge. *Id.* at 699. The patient arrived at the ER with severe headaches and saw an ER physician, who then consulted with the on-call neurologist. *Id.* The neurologist listened to the symptoms and diagnosed the patient with a "hemiplegic migraine." *Id.* The neurologist also stated, "No further treatment needs to be done for this patient." *Id.* The court determined that by listening to symptoms and making a diagnosis, the neurologist had evaluated the patient's information and made a medical decision. *Id.* These actions, the court reasoned, were affirmative acts to treat the patient and gave rise to a physician-patient relationship. *Id.*

Here, Dr. Antonio did not establish a physician-patient relationship because he did not take affirmative actions toward Navarro's treatment but only listened and sent her to another physician. When the ER physician contacted him, Dr. Antonio heard the symptoms and then responded with "This sounds gastrointestinal, not something I'm handling" followed by "I'm done here." The physician's acts are not affirmative acts to treat and therefore do not create a physician-patient relationship.

Although Dr. Antonio did appear to evaluate what the ER physician had told him, he did not pair that with an affirmative action nor did he indicate that he would further treat Navarro. When the ER physician called the second time, Dr. Antonio further insisted that he was not able to help by explicitly stating "I'm done here. I'm not doing this. This is outside my area completely."

Navarro may argue that by stating that the symptoms sounded more gastrointestinal than cardiac in nature, the physician implicitly made a diagnosis, namely that the condition was not a cardiac condition. Dr. Antonio suggested that the ER physician contact the gastrointestinal specialist. Even so, a simple referral to another specialty does not create a physician-patient relationship. *Id.* at 708. Dr. Antonio only opined on the symptoms so he could select another specialist for Navarro to see, not to treat the patient.

Thus, Dr. Antonio did not affirmatively act to treat the patient and made no medical decision, so Dr. Antonio likely did not establish a physician-patient relationship.

Exercise 42

 *Deeper Dive*

....

Skills Tested (explained on pages 92–93):

1. Structure (base arguments on rules)

2. Show Your Work (weave client facts and case information)

3. Nuts and Bolts (citation)

....

Examples: The sample memos in Chapter 8 contain examples of application sections (see pages 149, 155–56, 158–59).

Legal Principles:

> The Georgia Code defines false imprisonment as an unlawful detention of another, where the person is "deprived of his personal liberty" for any length of time. Ga. Code Ann. § 51-7-20.
>
> A detention may be physical but can also arise out of words, gestures, or other actions that give rise to a reasonable belief that force will be used if the plaintiff does not submit. *Smith v. Wal-Mart Stores E., LP*, 765 S.E.2d 518, 522 (Ga. Ct. App. 2014). If the defendant's actions operate on the will of the plaintiff and result in a reasonable fear of "personal difficulty or personal injuries," then the person is considered detained. *Id.*
>
> A young woman was detained in a store stockroom, for example, when a store manager accused her of stealing sunglasses and then led her to the stockroom. *Id.* The manager left the door unlocked and two inches ajar. *Id.* An armed security guard stood at the door and answered her queries about when she could leave with silence. *Id.* The guard remained standing in front of the slightly open door during the entire time that the woman was detained. *Id.* The woman said that she felt intimated by the guard, the weapon, and the uncertainty of what would happen if she tried to leave, so she stayed for forty-five minutes. *Id.* at 525. The manager said afterwards that the woman could have left any time she wanted. *Id.*
>
> Based on the guard's presence, the weapon, and the intimidation the woman felt, the woman was detained. *Id.*

Exercise: A person drafting an application section must decide whether to apply the rule directly or use analogical reasoning. The choice depends on the rule, the available law, and the complexity of the facts. In both scenarios below, the question is whether the person was detained. How will your application differ in the two scenarios set out below? Please write an application for both of the two different scenarios, using a central thesis statement and a topic sentence for each argument.

Scenario 1

Your client is Rick Bowman, who was accused of shoplifting snacks at a Bullseye store. The store security guard wrestled Bowman to the ground and then handcuffed him to a chair. Was Bowman detained?

Scenario 2

Your client is Sam Walker, who was accused of shoplifting toys from a Wow Toys store. A manager informed Walker that the security staff was reviewing videotapes, and the manager asked if Walker would stay during that process. "You can leave if you want," the manager said, "but if you leave, we'll call the police and ask that they arrest you. Most people stay and sort it out without the police. You probably don't want an arrest on your record." Walker said afterwards that he felt intimidated and afraid for his future, so he obeyed the manager.

Exercise 43

 *Deeper Dive*

Skills Tested (**explained on pages 92–93**):

1. Structure (thesis statement, arguments rather than cases, base arguments on rules, analysis parallels case illustration)
2. Effective Analogies (how to analogize, relevant comparisons)
3. Show Your Work (be specific, weave client facts and case information)
4. Nuts and Bolts (citation, objective tone)

Examples: The sample memos in Chapter 8 contain examples of application sections (see pages 149, 155–56, 158–59).

Factual Background: Shawna Fields is a senior at Central High School and plays on the varsity basketball team. She was disciplined for violating the school's dress code policy when she wore a tank top to school. This disciplinary issue made her ineligible to play in a college recruiting tournament, potentially costing her a college basketball scholarship. She sued Central High for violating her civil rights, arguing she did not violate the dress code and should not have been disciplined. The tank top in question is loose fitting, has one-inch straps across the shoulders, is not low cut, and does not show her stomach. It was clean when she wore it and had no holes or tears. The school's dress code provides as follows:

> ### Central High School Student Dress Code
>
> Students must wear clean, neat clothing that is appropriate for the classroom environment. CHS prohibits any clothing that is disruptive to the educational process or learning environment.
>
> CHS prohibits clothing that is revealing or sexually suggestive. Examples include but are not limited to:
>
> - Bare midriff tops
> - Halter tops, off-the-shoulder tops, or spaghetti strap tops
> - Tops that show cleavage
> - Swimwear or tube tops
> - Sleepwear

continued

> Students who do not meet these standards will be required to change clothing and are subject to discipline under CHS's Code of Student Conduct.

Legal Issue: Did Ms. Fields violate CHS's Student Dress Code by wearing a tank top?

Legal Background: This is the only court decision that has interpreted CHS's dress code:

> *Chute v. Smithville Indep. Sch. Dist.*, 982 N.W.2d 802, 805 (Mont. 2010).
>
> Mr. Chute's claim depends on proof that he violated Central High's Student Dress Code. The Code provides as follows: [omitted because it is identical to the Code quoted above].
>
> Mr. Chute was disciplined for wearing a muscle shirt to school. A muscle shirt is a sleeveless, collarless shirt, so called because it shows the wearer's entire arm, including the biceps. Mr. Chute's muscle shirt was neither form fitting nor loose fitting but fit like a standard-cut t-shirt, without the sleeves.
>
> CHS contends Mr. Chute violated the dress code by wearing the muscle shirt to school because the shirt bared his shoulders and is thus "revealing." We disagree. Considering the entire dress code in context establishes that it does not prohibit Mr. Chute from wearing a muscle shirt. The shirt was clean and neat, free from holes or signs of wear. There is no evidence that his shirt caused any disruption in CHS's educational or learning environment. Mr. Chute's shirt did expose the lower half of his shoulders, but that does not inherently render the shirt "revealing." The dress code does not ban all shoulder exposure but only the substantial exposure that would be present with halter, off-the-shoulder, spaghetti strap, or tube tops.
>
> We are not called on today to decide the propriety of the dress code, which seems to focus inordinately on female clothing. We hold only that, under the policy as written, Mr. Chute's muscle shirt is not "revealing" and does not otherwise violate CHS's Student Dress Code.

Exercise: Identify at least seven problems with the following application paragraph and then rewrite it to fix those problems. Assume this application paragraph follows both a paragraph with the relevant rule and subrule and a paragraph with a case illustration of *Chute*:

Ms. Fields will definitely win her case. There is no real difference between her case and Mr. Chute's case, and he won so she should too. Her tank top was not low cut, so it is crazy to say that the tank top was "revealing." It would be sex discrimination to say Ms. Fields violated the dress code but Mr. Chute didn't.

Exercise 44

 *Deeper Dive*

....

Skills Tested (explained on pages 92–93):

1. Structure (thesis statement, arguments rather than cases, base arguments on rules, analysis parallels case illustration)
2. Effective Analogies (how to analogize, relevant comparisons)
3. Show Your Work (be specific, weave client facts and case information, tie back to the rule)
4. Nuts and Bolts (citation)

....

Examples: The sample memos in Chapter 8 contain examples of application sections (see pages 149, 155–56, 158–59).

Factual Background: Carolyn and Bobby Simmons divorced when their only child, Natasha, was six months old. Bobby was awarded primary custody. On Carolyn's first visitation weekend after the divorce, she picked up Natasha but did not return at the appointed time the next day. Bobby began to panic and started looking for Carolyn and Natasha. He called and texted Carolyn's mother, Dorian McDonald, but she did not answer the calls or respond to his urgent texts. In the meantime, Carolyn had shown up at her mother's house the day before with Natasha and said she could not live only seeing her baby every other weekend. Dorian bought Carolyn some diapers and baby formula, gave her $250 in cash, and told her she did not want to know any details of whatever Carolyn was planning. Carolyn vanished with Natasha, and no one has heard from them since.

Legal Issue: Is Dorian liable under Chapter 42 of the Texas Family Code for assisting Carolyn in abducting the baby?

Exercise: The discussion section of your memo begins with the following two paragraphs, which state a conclusion, provide the rules, and give a case illustration.

Ms. McDonald likely assisted Ms. Simmons in abducting the baby. The Texas Family Code provides a cause of action against a person "who takes or retains possession of a child or who conceals the whereabouts of a child in violation of the possessory rights of another." Tex. Fam. Code Ann. § 42.002(a). In addition to this claim against the person who takes or conceals a child, the Family Code provides a cause of action against anyone "who aids or assists" the person in taking or concealing a child. *Id.* § 42.003(a). Aid can be direct or indirect, so long as the person providing it can fairly to be said to be assisting in the taking or concealing of the child. *See Lambert v. Fitch*, 15 S.W.3d 339, 341 (Tex. 2001).

Providing financial and material support to the abductor is evidence of assistance. *Id.* In *Lambert*, Mr. Lambert's sister took out a $3,000 loan and gave him the money a week before he abducted his child from school. *Id.* The sister also bought the child new clothes and toys and drove the child and her brother to the airport, where he fled with his son to Mexico. *Id.* The child's mother called the sister to see if she had seen the child or Mr. Lambert, and the sister did not return her calls. *Id.* When the truth eventually came to light, the mother sued Mr. Lambert's sister for assisting him in abducting the child, and the jury found in the mother's favor. *Id.* The court found that the evidence was sufficient to support the verdict. *Id.* Taking out the loan before the abduction allowed the jury to infer that she knew about his plans in advance. *Id.* Moreover, giving Mr. Lambert money and supplies as well as a ride to the airport directly aided the abduction, as did slowing the mother's efforts to find the child by refusing to communicate with her. *Id.*

The chart below contains sentences that could be part of the application that would follow the above paragraphs. For each sentence, first determine whether it should be included. Then, for the ones that should be included, determine whether they are missing specific facts that would be helpful. Explain your reasoning.

continued

APPLICATION SENTENCES
(1) Based on her daughter's statement about not being able to live only seeing the baby on weekends and the financial and material support she provided thereafter, a jury could infer that Ms. McDonald knew her daughter intended to abduct the baby, just as Mr. Lambert's sister knew of his intention and took out a loan a week in advance to have travel money to give him. *Id.*
(2) Mr. Lambert's sister took out a loan in advance, gave him the money, gave him clothes for the child, took him to the airport, and refused to call back the child's mother, just as Ms. McDonald knew her daughter was distraught over the custody arrangements, gave her money, gave her diapers and formula, and would not return the mother's calls or texts.
(3) Ms. McDonald gave her daughter money and supplies, which parallels Mr. Lambert's sister providing him with money and supplies.
(4) Thus, based on Ms. Simmons's statements to Ms. McDonald and the money and supplies she gave her daughter, Ms. McDonald likely assisted in the abduction.
(5) Like the defendant's sister in *Lambert*, Ms. McDonald assisted in the abduction by giving her daughter money and provisions for the baby, knowing her daughter intended to abduct the baby.
(6) Mr. Lambert's sister took him to the airport, but Ms. McDonald did not take her daughter anywhere.
(7) And both the defendant here and in *Lambert* impeded the other parent's ability to locate the child by refusing to communicate. *Id.*
(8) The defendant was liable in *Lambert* when she helped an abductor, so Ms. McDonald should be liable too.

Counterargument and Rebuttal

Summary of Skills Tested

A legal memo focuses on arguments that support the writer's conclusion, also known as the affirmative argument. But the memo should also tackle the strongest argument (or arguments) opposing that conclusion: the counterargument. The counterargument immediately follows the affirmative argument. After the counterargument, the rebuttal shows conclusively why the counterargument fails.

Structure. The counterargument should contain the same type of specific legal and factual support as the affirmative argument; the particular content and level of detail depend on the specific issue. Once the writer has fully explained the counterargument, next comes a clear shift to rebuttal. The rebuttal should respond directly and explicitly to the counterargument. Discrete counterarguments are set out and rebutted separately.

SKILLS TESTED IN THIS CHAPTER	
SKILL	EXERCISE
Structure	46, 47, 48
Substance	45, 46, 47, 48
Clear Transition	46, 47, 48

Substance. A counterargument should consist of the *strongest* viable attack on the affirmative argument; the memo's reader needs to be fully informed about the affirmative argument's true vulnerabilities. A hasty writer may be tempted to make do with a "straw man"—or baseless—argument, due to the ease with which it is dispatched. But such arguments have no place in a useful legal memo. The counterargument should be drafted with the same rigor, logic, and attention as the affirmative argument.

No new law should appear in the counterargument; the counterargument should be written and rebutted using law that the writer explained earlier.

Finally, the rebuttal should not simply restate the affirmative argument but should provide some layer of detail or nuance not stated before, to reaffirm the writer's prediction.

Clear Transitions. The counterargument and rebuttal involve shifts from one side of the argument to the other, and then back again in the rebuttal. Without signposts, the reader can become disoriented, unsure of which side the writer is arguing. The writer, therefore, should flag each shift with signposting words such as "on the other hand." As the writer continues to argue in opposition to the main conclusion, the writer can orient the reader by noting occasionally that such a counterargument is "arguably" so. Following these signposting conventions, the writer can explain and rebut the counterargument without leaving the reader adrift.

The memo's reader will appreciate a deft treatment of the strongest arguments against the memo's main conclusion. Read on to try your hand at writing—and rebutting—a useful counterargument. You will find annotated sample answers to the even-numbered exercises at the back of this book. The sample memos in Chapter 8 include examples of counterarguments and rebuttals that apply these skills.

Exercise 45

(15) *Lightning Round*

....

Skill Tested (explained on pages 119–20):

Substance (only viable counterarguments, no new law)

....

Examples: The sample memos in Chapter 8 contain examples of counterarguments and rebuttals (see pages 149–50, 156–57, 159).

Factual Background: Ryan Beasley's dog Pepper loves going for walks on the neighborhood path that is full of children and other dog walkers. Ryan always keeps Pepper on a leash because Pepper sometimes gets excited. Almost every time they go out for a walk, Pepper lunges and growls at passers-by and will even snap at them. One evening during their walk, Pepper suddenly lunged toward a woman, Gloria King, who was walking her dog. The leash slipped from Ryan's hands, and Pepper got away and attacked Gloria and her dog, injuring both. Pepper had never attacked another dog or any person and had never bitten anyone before. Gloria sued Ryan for negligence.

Legal Background: In Florida, a dog owner can be liable for injuries to others if the owner knew or had reason to know of the dog's dangerous propensities and failed to take reasonable measures to protect others from the dog. *Marshall v. Higginbotham*, 212 So. 3d 219, 221 (Fla. 2017). Florida has firmly rejected the one-bite rule, meaning that a prior bite is not necessary to establish knowledge of a dog's dangerous propensities. *See id.*

Legal Issue: Is Ryan subject to liability to Gloria for the injuries Pepper caused?

Exercise: You have written an application paragraph of a memo concluding that Ryan is likely subject to liability for Pepper's attack. You reason that Pepper's frequent aggressive behavior, including snapping and lunging, put Ryan on notice that Pepper was dangerous. You further argue that the use of a leash, standing alone, was not a reasonable protective measure for a dog known to be aggressive on a busy neighborhood path. Now the counterargument and rebuttal must be addressed. Is Option A or Option B the better counterargument and rebuttal? Please explain your reasoning.

continued

Option A

Mr. Beasley will likely emphasize that Pepper had never bitten anyone before and so he could not possibly have known that Pepper would actually attack someone if unrestrained. *See Townsend v. Levy*, 485 S.W.3d 901, 904 (Tex. App. 2016) (holding that owner could not, as a matter of law, have foreseen her dog's attack on a child because the dog had never bitten before). This argument will fail because unlike the non-binding Texas authority cited, Florida does not follow the one-bite rule, which means that an owner can be aware of a dog's dangerous propensities for reasons other than a prior bite. *See Marshall*, 212 So. 3d at 221. Pepper's near-constant lunging and snapping during these walks was sufficient to alert Mr. Beasley of the need to take appropriate measures to protect others on the neighborhood path from Pepper, meaning Mr. Beasley is likely subject to liability for Pepper's conduct.

Option B

Mr. Beasley will likely argue that he took appropriate protective measures by ensuring Pepper was leashed on every walk and that it was not his fault that the leash slipped from his hand. A court is likely to reject this argument because it is foreseeable that aggressive behavior could make Pepper hard to restrain. Pepper lunges frequently, and a leash slipping is not an extraordinary event in such circumstances. Mr. Beasley should have taken additional protective measures, such as using a muzzle. Thus, Mr. Beasley is likely subject to liability for Pepper's conduct.

Exercise 46

Lightning Round

> **Skills Tested (explained on pages 119–20):**
> 1. Structure (detail the counterarguments, explicitly rebut)
> 2. Substance (rebut with new analysis)
> 3. Clear Transitions

Examples: The sample memos in Chapter 8 contain examples of counterarguments and rebuttals (see pages 149–50, 156–57, 159).

Factual Background: After running some errands, Grant Coulson was with his two young children in a shopping center parking lot. Daisy, his infant, was strapped into a baby carrier, and he held hands with Leo, his three-year-old son. When Grant arrived at his car, he let go of Leo and instructed him, as per their usual procedure, to hold onto his leg while he removed Daisy from the baby carrier and strapped her into her car seat. Daisy began to struggle and cry, so Grant took longer than usual to get her strapped in. Meanwhile, Leo had let go of his father's leg, but Grant did not realize this because his attention was on Daisy. Grant heard an odd thumping sound but did not know what it was until, about fifteen seconds later, he heard someone exclaim, "Oh no, what have I done?" He then noticed Leo was not holding onto his leg, and fearing the worst, he turned around to see Leo unconscious on the pavement in front of a car that he realized had just hit Leo. Leo survived, but he has a permanent brain injury. It turns out that the car's driver, Jemma Johnson, had been texting while driving and had not seen Leo before she hit him. Grant sued Johnson on behalf of Leo for negligence and sued Johnson on his own behalf for negligent infliction of emotional distress on a bystander theory of recovery.

Legal Background: In Texas, generally no claim exists for negligent infliction of emotional distress. *Chapa v. Traciers & Assocs.*, 267 S.W.3d 386, 398 (Tex. App. 2008). However, an exception exists for a bystander who suffers emotional distress for the contemporaneous and sensory perception of a serious or fatal injury to a close relative. *Id.* To prevail on a bystander claim, the plaintiff must meet three conditions: (1) the plaintiff must have been at or near the scene of the accident, (2) the plaintiff must have a direct emotional impact from "the sensory and contemporaneous observation of the accident," and (3) the plaintiff and the victim must be closely related. *Id.* If the facts are undisputed, then whether the plaintiff can recover as a bystander is a question of law. *Id.*

Legal Issue: Can Grant recover against Jemma as a bystander?

Exercise: You have been asked to write a memo focusing only on the second condition, whether Grant had a sensory and contemporaneous observation of the event. Because Leo was Grant's son and Grant was at the accident scene, the other elements are met. You have written an application paragraph of a memo concluding that this element is probably not met because Grant heard a sound but did not know what it was until after the accident was over and thus did not contemporaneously perceive the accident. Now the counterargument and rebuttal must be addressed. The chart below contains some sentences that could be used for a counterargument and rebuttal. Decide which ones are needed for a counterargument and rebuttal paragraph relating to the above factual background and legal issue and which order the necessary items should be in. Explain your reasoning.

SENTENCES
(1) Even so, a court will probably reject this argument.
(2) Coulson did not see the accident, and so he cannot recover as a bystander as a matter of law, no matter what he saw after the accident.
(3) Thus, because Coulson observed only the aftermath of the accident and not the accident itself, he probably cannot meet the second condition for bystander recovery.
(4) Coulson did not know that the thump he heard was anything troubling until he heard the driver's exclamation, and by that point, the accident was over.
(5) Coulson will argue that he contemporaneously experienced with his sense of hearing an unusual sound and within seconds saw Leo unconscious on the pavement after being hit by a car.
(6) Because a bystander claim is an exception to the general rule against negligent infliction of emotional distress claims, a court will probably construe it narrowly to avoid the exception swallowing the rule.
(7) This argument will fail.
(8) He will likely emphasize that although he did not see the accident, sensorial perception by its very terms includes senses other than vision; that another sense, here his hearing, took a few seconds to process the incident does not make his perception of the accident any less contemporaneous.

5,7,8,1,4,3,6,2

Exercise 47

 *Deeper Dive*

Skills Tested (explained on pages 119–20):

1. Structure (detail the counterarguments, separate multiple counter-arguments, explicitly rebut)
2. Substance (only viable counterarguments, rebut with new analysis)
3. Clear Transitions

Examples: The sample memos in Chapter 8 contain examples of counterarguments and rebuttals (see pages 149–50, 156–57, 159).

Factual Background: Porsha is a social media influencer; her husband Anthony has a master's degree in art and is pursuing a fledgling career as a sculptor. Porsha and Anthony fell in love and decided to marry, but Porsha refused to marry Anthony unless he signed a prenuptial agreement, and Anthony agreed. The agreement limited Anthony to a single payment of $50,000 if they divorced. Before they signed the agreement, Porsha and Anthony disclosed their assets to one another. Porsha had a net worth of around $1 million while Anthony's was around $100,000. Porsha and Anthony were married in Georgia; the marriage lasted two years. Anthony filed for divorce after discovering Porsha had been having an affair. When Anthony was moving out and the two were dividing their belongings, he came across a trunk in the attic and opened it. To his shock, it contained several antique vases that he knew, because of his art background, were worth at least a half a million dollars collectively. Porsha had never mentioned these vases. She said she forgot to tell him about them during the asset disclosure because she had inherited the trunk when her grandmother died ten years earlier; Porsha thought the contents were junk. Anthony now seeks to invalidate the prenuptial agreement on the ground that Porsha did not disclose all of her material assets and that if he had known about the vases, he would not have signed.

Legal Background: In Georgia, prenuptial agreements are not invalid as a matter of law but can be declared unenforceable on several grounds, including the nondisclosure of a material asset. *See Scherer v. Scherer*, 292 S.E.2d 662, 640 (Ga. 1982). There must be "a full and fair disclosure" of all assets prior to executing a prenuptial agreement. *See Blige v. Blige*, 656 S.E.2d 822, 825 (Ga. 2008). A nondisclosure is material if it would have been a critical factor in the opposing spouse's decision. *See Corbett v. Corbett*, 628 S.E.2d 585, 586 (Ga. 2006). The law does not impose a duty to inquire about assets; each side has an affirmative obligation to disclose. *See Blige*, 656 S.E.2d at 826.

Legal Issue: Is the prenuptial agreement unenforceable because Porsha did not disclose the vases?

Exercise: You have written an application paragraph of a memo concluding that the agreement is likely unenforceable based on nondisclosure of a material asset. You have reasoned that the vases are a significant asset, and because Anthony said he would not have entered into the agreement had he known of their existence, the agreement is unenforceable. Now you must address the counterargument and rebuttal. Below is a series of sentences that, together, will form a counterargument and rebuttal. For each sentence, there are two choices. Which one in each set is best suited to a counterargument and rebuttal based on the facts and law set out above? What is wrong with the other ones?

I. *Sentence One*

 A.   The agreement might be enforceable.

 B.   Porsha could argue that failing to disclose the vases was not a material nondisclosure.

II. *Sentence Two*

 A.   Arguably, because Porsha did not remember she had the vases, she did not choose to deceive Anthony or otherwise induce him into signing the agreement based on incomplete information.

 B.   She did not remember the vases, so their omission was unintentional, and he never asked her about anything such as vases or art.

III. *Sentence Three*

 A.   This argument will likely fail.

 B.   The agreement is unenforceable.

IV. *Sentence Four*

 A.   Even though she might not have intended to withhold material information, she nevertheless did. The law on this point looks at the extent of the pre-agreement disclosures, not the discloser's intent. *See Blige*, 656 S.E.2d at 825. The nondisclosure here was material based both on the asset's high value and Anthony's statement that he would not have signed the agreement if he had known about the vases.

 B.   Anthony would not have signed the agreement if he had known about the vases.

V. *Sentence Five*

 A.   The agreement is unenforceable.

 B.   Thus, the agreement is likely unenforceable, despite Porsha's protestations that her nondisclosure was accidental.

Exercise 48

 *Deeper Dive*

....

Skills Tested (explained on pages 119–20):

1. Structure (detail the counterarguments, explicitly rebut)
2. Substance (rebut with new analysis)
3. Clear Transitions

....

Examples: The sample memos in Chapter 8 contain examples of counterarguments and rebuttals (see pages 149–50, 156–57, 159).

Factual Background: Dana Mulder was severely injured in a car accident. She was driving a 2017 Wesla Model 3, and the airbag malfunctioned by failing to deploy. When the car was inspected post-accident, the airbag showed error code 55. Error code 55 arises from a faulty link in one of two separate connectors—connector A and connector B—leading to the airbag. Each connector serves an independent function. Expert testimony undisputedly establishes that the code 55 error in this case related to connector A. Mulder has sued your client, Wesla, alleging that the airbag was negligently designed. She seeks to admit at trial a spreadsheet showing warranty claims for all airbag error code 55 incidents on 2017 Wesla Model 3s. The spreadsheet contains 78 entries spanning two years. One column on the spreadsheet contains information about which connector was involved, and it shows 33 connector A claims, 18 connector B claims, and 27 claims where that column was left blank.

Legal Background: In a products liability action, evidence of other similar incidents may be relevant if the incidents "occurred under reasonably similar (though not necessarily identical) conditions." *ABC Motors v. Smith*, 422 S.W.3d 901, 905 (Tenn. 2015). The party seeking to admit the evidence bears the burden of establishing substantial similarity. *Id.*

Legal Issue: Is the spreadsheet admissible as evidence of other similar incidents?

Exercise: You have written an application paragraph of a memo concluding that a court is likely to admit the portion of the spreadsheet relating to the connector A claims but not the remaining parts of the spreadsheet. You reasoned that the specific defect mechanism, here the connector A for error code 55, must be the same for the other incidents to be relevant. Because the connector B mechanism is not the same and the connector involved for incidents in which the connector column was left blank is unknown, Ms. Mulder cannot show sufficient similarity. The following is a counterargument and rebuttal paragraph that would follow your analysis. Identify five specific problems and then rewrite the paragraph to address those concerns.

> The other entries on the spreadsheet are relevant. They are all about error code 55, and that is close enough since the other incidents do not need to be identical. But a court would probably disagree with this because they are not identical.

Chapter 6

Memo Conclusion

Summary of Skills Tested

The conclusion section wraps up the memo, providing a high-level summary of each issue's outcome.

Keep It Short; Give the Reasons. The conclusion should be brief, yet it should give the basis for each outcome.

Consistency. The conclusion should raise no new issues, and the conclusion's content should be consistent with the memo's main content. For example, the type and strength of the conclusion's prediction language should match what was included in the introduction, brief answer, and analysis.

Give Any Advice. In the course of researching and writing a memo, a writer may learn information or have an important idea that is not directly responsive to the question asked. For example, the writer may realize the need to develop additional facts or to raise new claims or defenses. In that case, the writer can include the information or advice in the conclusion.

| SKILLS TESTED IN THIS CHAPTER ||
SKILL	EXERCISE
Keep It Short	49, 50
Give the Reasons	49, 50
Consistency	49, 50
Give Any Advice	49, 50
Nuts and Bolts	49, 50

Nuts and Bolts. An effective conclusion is direct, giving the outcome immediately. The conclusion does not generally include citations.

These exercises will show you how to write a conclusion that closes your memo appropriately. Annotated sample answers to the even-numbered exercises are at the back of this book. For examples of memo conclusion sections, refer to the sample memos in Chapter 8.

Exercise 49

 *Lightning Round*

....

Skills Tested (explained on page 129):

1. Keep It Short
2. Give the Reasons
3. Consistency
4. Give Any Advice
5. Nuts and Bolts (answer immediately)

....

Examples: The sample memos in Chapter 8 contain examples of memo conclusion sections (see pages 150, 160).

Exercise: Your memo addresses whether a particular land use satisfies the open and notorious conduct element required for adverse possession. The memo contains the following brief answer:

> Probably not. To establish the open and notorious element of adverse possession, a claimant's use must be plainly visible, creating a presumption of notice to the title owner. GasNow's gas pipes on the Martinez property were not visible to the naked eye because they were underground. Although GasNow also installed metal plates at thirty-foot intervals along the pipe's route, those too were not easily visible unless the owner stood close to or above them. Thus, GasNow's use of the Martinez property probably does not satisfy the open and notorious element of adverse possession because an ordinary owner would not easily see GasNow's use.

Based on this brief answer, which conclusion is more effective? Please give at least three reasons why.

POTENTIAL CONCLUSIONS
(1) GasNow's use of the property almost certainly will not constitute the requisite open and notorious conduct for an adverse possession claim.
(2) GasNow's use of the property probably will not satisfy the open and notorious element of adverse possession because GasNow's pipes were hidden underground and its metal plates were only visible from very close up.
(3) GasNow's use of the property probably will not satisfy the open and notorious element of adverse possession because GasNow's pipes were hidden underground and its metal plates were only visible from very close up. On the other hand, GasNow could argue that because the metal plates were both numerous and shiny, the use is sufficient to be considered open and notorious. This argument will probably fail, as even numerous and shiny plates are hard to spot from afar when they are flush with the ground.

Exercise 50

 *Lightning Round*

Examples: The sample memos in Chapter 8 contain examples of memo conclusion sections (see pages 150, 160).

Exercise: Your memo contains the following introduction:

> Leah Beety sued our client, Big K Groceries, after she slipped and fell in a puddle of spilled coffee in one of Big K's stores. This claim will likely fail because Big K did not breach any duty and because the fall did not cause Beety's damages.

The body of the memo then provides the facts, rules, and legal analysis to support these conclusions. The chart below contains some sentences that you should consider whether to include in the conclusion section of the memo. Decide which ones are needed. Explain why each should or should not be included.

POTENTIAL CONCLUSION SECTION SENTENCES
(1) Beety's claim against Big K will fail.
(2) Beety's claim against Big K will likely fail on both the breach of duty and causation elements. Because Big K cleaned the floor regularly and the coffee spill she slipped on had been on the floor for only one minute, Big K likely did not breach any duty. Further, Beety injured her back in a car accident a month before she slipped in the store, so the car accident, not the slip, likely caused her damages.

(3) Liability flows from conduct that causes reasonably foreseeable harm. *Bossley v. Smith*, 555 S.W.3d 290, 295 (Tex. 2018). A harm is foreseeable if a person of ordinary intelligence should have reasonably anticipated the danger. *Id.*

(4) Big K also probably owed Beety no duty as a matter of law because the condition that caused her fall—a spilled cup of coffee brought in from outside the store—was not within Big K's control.

(5) We may also have a good argument that Big K owed Beety no duty as a matter of law because the condition that caused her fall—a spilled cup of coffee brought in from outside the store—was not within Big K's control. If you would like me to research and analyze this issue, please let me know.

Chapter 7

Email Memos

Summary of Skills Tested

Some clients or assigning attorneys seek the answer to a legal question but may not need a complete memo. Under such circumstances, an email memo may suffice. An email memo contains the essential parts of the legal analysis but in a truncated format suitable for email transmission. Use the conventions described below to draft an informative and user-friendly email memo.

Format. An email memo works best with short sentences and paragraphs. Headings and labels, including enumeration, will help the reader quickly understand the point and move between topics or sections of the email. Use more white space than usual, so the reader is not bogged down in dense blocks of text. All these techniques make the message much more readable on a screen, where the recipient will most likely be viewing the email memo.

Language. The email memo is less formal than a full memo. The writer should still, however, use a professional tone. Proper grammar, punctuation, and mechanics remain essential. Writers should avoid contractions in the full memo but may use them in an email memo. The writer should not adopt idiosyncratic or overly familiar abbreviations, such as those that might be seen in personal messages. Do not include emoticons.

SKILLS TESTED IN THIS CHAPTER	
SKILL	EXERCISE
Format	51, 52, 53, 54
Language	51, 53, 54
Content	51, 53, 54

Content. Begin email memos with a specific, descriptive subject line so that the reader immediately knows the contents and importance of your message before even opening it. Ensure your email memo is concise and efficient. The introduction paragraph should, after perhaps a very short personal statement if appropriate in the context, state the point of the message, your conclusion, and any immediate action items. Keep the factual descriptions and analysis concise and to the point; aim to fit the message on one computer screen. Rather than including extensive case illustrations, an email memo generally uses rule-based analysis or, at most, a summary of a particularly useful case. Citations should be sparse.

The exercises that follow will help you develop appropriate and helpful email memos. Annotated sample answers to the even-numbered exercises are in the back of this book.

Exercise 51

 *Lightning Round*

Skills Tested (explained on pages 135–36):

1. Format (short sentences and paragraphs, white space)
2. Language (professional, grammatical)
3. Content (specific subject line, concise, efficient)

Factual Background: You are a summer associate at a large law firm. Last night, you attended a recruiting event at a pool hall and met a partner, Cristina Trujillo, who gave you an assignment. She asked you to research Texas law to determine whether a bystander can assert a claim for negligent infliction of emotional distress and email her the answer sometime the next day.

Exercise: Below is a draft of an email to the partner. Please identify eight specific problems with the draft and suggest how to fix them.

> Subject: Follow up
>
> Hey Cristina! It was so great meeting you last night at Slick Willie's. My pool-shooting skills need some work, but it was fun trying!! You were really good where did you learn to play like that. ☺ I'm so honored that you asked me to do some research for you. You wanted to know about Texas law and about how if a bystander wants to assert a claim for negligent infliction of emotional distress if the bystander can do that. The answer is yes. Just look at this attached law review article, which explains all about it. I admire you so much and hope this is the first of many collaborations to come. Thx for the opportunity. Have a blessed day, Jasmine

Exercise 52

 *Lightning Round*

Skill Tested (explained on page 135):

> Format (short sentences and paragraphs, headings and labels, white space)

Exercise: The following email memo excerpt contains appropriate content, but some formatting adjustments, including headings, would make it much easier to read and absorb on a screen, particularly a small one. Review the email memo excerpt, identify the problems, and suggest how to fix them.

Dear Ms. Maddux,

You asked me to analyze whether our client, Mr. Burger, could be vicariously liable for the conduct of its employee in assaulting a customer. Mr. Burger would likely not be vicariously liable because the employee was acting outside the course and scope of his employment when he angrily assaulted a customer. Johnny Hudson worked for Mr. Burger, taking orders and serving food. Austin Parks, a Mr. Burger customer, became upset when he did not have his food ten minutes after placing his order. Parks started berating Hudson, who was working behind the counter and had taken Parks's order. Hudson responded by throwing a milkshake blender at Parks, hitting him in the head. Parks has sued Hudson and Mr. Burger, asserting Mr. Burger is vicariously liable for Parks's assault. Employers can be vicariously liable for a worker's tort if the worker is (1) an employee, (2) acting in the course and scope of employment, (3) at the time of the tortious conduct. *Wisenhouse v. Armendez*, 14 S.W.3d 200, 201 (Tex. App. 2000). Hudson was on shift working for Mr. Burger when he threw the milkshake blender at Parks, and thus the timing element is not an issue. This memo will address whether Hudson was an employee at the time of the assault and, if so, whether he was acting in the course and scope of his employment when he assaulted Parks. Hudson was likely a Mr. Burger employee because Mr. Burger controlled all essential details of Hudson's work. Because Hudson acted out of anger and not to further Mr. Burger's business, however, Hudson was probably not acting in the course and scope of his employment, and thus Mr. Burger will probably not be vicariously liable for his conduct. [Additional analysis would be included about each of these two elements.]

Exercise 53

 *Deeper Dive*

....

Skills Tested (explained on pages 135–36):

1. Format (short sentences and paragraphs)

2. Language (less formal, professional)

3. Content (specific subject line, concise, efficient, rule-based analysis, few cites)

....

Factual Background: Alexander Waugh, a man from the Pacific Islands, worked for our client, Old Army, as a retail sales associate. He was fired after he violated company policy by being late for work twice and failing to punch in his timecard once. He filed a race discrimination lawsuit against Old Army, and his main evidence of discrimination is that two Hispanic employees who were also late were not fired.

Exercise: You were asked to write an email memo analyzing Waugh's claim based on his evidence comparing himself to other employees. Below is a series of sentences that could be included in your email memo. Which one in each set is best suited to an email memo on your assignment? What is wrong with the other ones?

I. *Subject Line*

   A.   Waugh's Termination Claim

   B.   Analysis re: Whether Waugh Is Similarly Situated to Hispanic Employees

II. *Introduction*

   A.   You asked me to analyze Waugh's claim that he was discriminated against based on his race, Pacific Islander, because two Hispanic employees were not fired for being late. Waugh likely isn't similarly situated to these employees because he committed more or more serious infractions.

   B.   I've completed the research and analysis you requested on whether Waugh is similarly situated to two Hispanic employees who were not fired after they were late for work. What follows is my analysis of this issue.

III. *Rules Explanation 1*

   A.   To establish a prima facie case of termination based on racial discrimination in employment, the plaintiff must show: (1) he is a member of a protected class, (2) he was qualified for the position, (3) he was fired, and (4) he was treated less favorably because of his race as compared to other similarly situated employees of a different race under nearly identical circumstances. *See Lee v. Kansas City S. Ry. Co.*, 574 F.3d 253, 259 (5th Cir. 2009). Once an employee makes out a prima facie case, an inference of discrimination is raised, and the burden of production shifts to the employer. *See id.* The employer must then offer a legitimate, non-discriminatory reason for its action. *See id.* If the employer does so, the inference of discrimination disappears, and the burden shifts back to the employee to prove that the employer's explanation for the termination is a pretext for discrimination. *See id.* When considering whether employees are similarly situated, employees who have different work responsibilities or who are disciplined for dissimilar infractions are not sufficiently similar for comparison. *See id.* at 259–60.

B.   To prove termination based on race discrimination, a plaintiff must prove, among other things, that he was treated less favorably than similarly situated employees of a different race under nearly identical circumstances. When considering whether employees are similarly situated, employees who are disciplined for dissimilar infractions are not sufficiently similar. *See Lee v. Kansas City S. Ry. Co.*, 574 F.3d 253, 259–60 (5th Cir. 2009).

IV. *Rules Explanation 2*

A.   For example, two employees accused of theft were not similarly situated to a plaintiff fired for theft because the plaintiff's theft was more serious. The plaintiff worked for a food services operation that catered a bar mitzvah. He was fired for allegedly stealing a cash envelope from the gift table. He claimed discrimination, arguing that two other employees of a different race stole alcohol and decorations but were not fired. The court concluded that the comparators were not similarly situated because their theft of company supplies was not as serious as the plaintiff's theft from the client, which could damage the company's reputation and subject it to civil liability. *See Bryant v. Compass Grp. USA Inc.*, 413 F.3d 471, 474, 478 (5th Cir. 2005).

B.   *See Bryant v. Compass Grp. USA Inc.*, 413 F.3d 471, 474, 478 (5th Cir. 2005) (holding that the comparators were not similarly situated when the plaintiff stole from a company client, potentially damaging the company's reputation and subjecting it to civil liability, whereas the comparators stole only from the company itself).

V. *Analysis*

    A.   Waugh points to two Hispanic employees, Daniels and Rubio, who also violated Old Army's attendance policy but were not fired. Daniels, however, was late only once, whereas Waugh was late twice and had another infraction for failing to punch his timecard. Rubio was thirty minutes late three times, but she notified her supervisor in advance, and her tardiness was due to medical appointments. Waugh, on the other hand, came to work two hours late twice, with no notice or explanation, causing substantial workplace disruption. Thus, Waugh was not disciplined under nearly identical circumstances as Daniels and Rubio, and so Waugh was not similarly situated to them.

    B.   Waugh points to two Hispanic employees, Daniels and Rubio, who also violated Old Army's attendance policy but were not fired. However, their circumstances were different, and so they weren't similarly situated to Waugh.

VI. *Conclusion*

    A.   Let me know if you need anything else.

    B.   Based on a comparison to the other employees Waugh identifies, Waugh likely won't be able to meet his burden to show similarly situated employees of a different race were treated more favorably. This could provide the basis for a strong summary judgment motion for our client. If you have any questions or would like me to prepare a summary judgment motion, please let me know.

Exercise 54

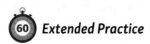 *Extended Practice*

Skills Tested (explained on pages 135–36):

1. Format (short sentences and paragraphs, headings and labels, white space)

2. Language (less formal, professional, grammatical)

3. Content (specific subject line, concise, efficient, rule-based analysis, few cites)

Exercise: Convert the single-issue memo in Chapter 8 (see pages 145–50) into an email memo.

Sample Memos (with Annotations)

This chapter features two full-length memos that demonstrate the skills explored throughout the book. The memos are samples, meaning that they represent one way to carry out the skills; they do not represent the only way to do so. Each memo is annotated, so readers can see which skills are shown in the various parts of the memos.

Single-Issue Memo. The first memo in this chapter is a single-issue memo containing all traditional memo parts: the heading, introduction, question presented, brief answer, statement of facts, discussion, and conclusion. Any assigning person might wish to subtract from this list of parts, perhaps omitting the introduction, for example. Legal writers should defer to their assigning person's preferences.

Two-Issue Memo. The second memo in this chapter addresses two separate legal issues. The two-issue memo contains the same parts as the single-issue memo, with adjustments required when more than one issue is addressed.

A writer addressing two legal issues in the same memo must treat the issues together in some sections and distinctly in others. For example, the introduction points out both issues and gives a conclusion for each. The question presented and brief answer for each issue, however, will generally be distinct. When possible, the statement of facts will contain a single narrative for both issues. The discussion section should begin with a roadmap that orients the reader to the two issues that follow. The roadmap typically includes the conclusion for each issue, an overall rule for each issue, and any overarching concerns that affect the analysis of both. Sometimes a memo's circumstances might call for a different approach. For example, a roadmap might not include overall rules if several unrelated issues have distinct overall rules and including them all in the roadmap would be unwieldy.

After the roadmap, each separate issue is treated in its own unit of analysis. The memo conclusion section should contain the conclusion for each issue, together with any suitable advice for the reader.

Use the sample memos however you see fit—perhaps when embarking on a new memo skill, to see how that skill looks in a complete memo. Or try reading the sample memos in their entirety, taking in the flow from one section to the next.

MEMORANDUM

TO: Carole Maldonado, Supervising Attorney

FROM: Joe Finlay, Summer Associate

DATE: October 1, 2020

RE: The reasonableness of Elaine Swift's request to bring in outside food to Fun Zone (client/ matter number 001632.0001)

> The **Heading** contains the recipient, author, current date, and a brief statement of the specific issue; it is aligned and has ample white space

I. Introduction

> The **Introduction** sets out the client, the specific issue, a reference to the rule, the conclusion, and the basis for the conclusion

Our client, eight-year-old Elaine Swift, has sued Fun Zone, Inc., in the Southern District of Texas for disability discrimination under the Americans with Disabilities Act (ADA). Elaine has severe food allergies and cannot safely eat any of Fun Zone's food. She thus asked that Fun Zone modify its policies to allow her to bring in the food for the birthday party she wanted to hold there. Fun Zone refused. The ADA requires certain businesses such as Fun Zone to make reasonable modifications to accommodate individuals with disabilities under some circumstances. As you requested, this memorandum addresses only whether Elaine will be able to prove that the modification she requested—to bring in outside food—was reasonable. Elaine offered to bring the food in herself rather than demanding that Fun Zone prepare safe food, and sharing food with her guests is an important part of the party experience. Thus, Elaine will likely be able to establish that her request was reasonable as a general matter, which is all that this element requires.

II. Question Presented

Under the Americans with Disabilities Act, which requires certain businesses to make reasonable modifications to accommodate individuals with disabilities unless doing so would fundamentally alter the nature of the business, was Elaine's request for Fun Zone to modify its no-outside-food policy because of her food allergies reasonable?

> The **Question Presented** follows an accepted format, raises the precise question, and gives the legal context with some specific facts; it is readable and concise

III. Brief Answer

> The **Brief Answer** quickly answers the question, echoes the question language, and follows the Conclusion-Rule-Application-Conclusion format

Likely yes. A requested modification need only be generally reasonable in the run of cases, and that is assessed case by case, considering the nature of the disability and the burden on the defendant. Elaine could die if she eats Fun Zone's

> The question presented and brief answer work together to give the reader a concise, standalone overview of the key facts, law, and analysis

food, and allowing her to bring in the food for the entire party ensures that she can eat safely and fit in with her friends, giving her the same type of party experience as a non-allergic child. Thus, her request for Fun Zone to modify its policy against outside food was likely reasonable.

IV.   Statement of Facts

Elaine Swift is an eight-year-old girl with multiple, severe food allergies. Fun Zone, Inc., is a popular birthday party destination that serves food and drinks and has a big gaming area. Elaine sued Fun Zone for disability discrimination after Fun Zone refused to allow her to bring in her own food to accommodate her food allergies, meaning Elaine could not safely have a birthday party at Fun Zone.

The Statement of Facts begins by orienting the reader to the parties and current issue

Elaine is severely allergic to peanuts, tree nuts, eggs, wheat, and dairy products. If she ingests even a trace of one of these allergens, she could have an allergic reaction so severe that she might die. It is dangerous for Elaine to eat any food prepared in a kitchen that serves one of her allergens because of the risk that some of the allergen can be transferred to her food from sources such as the hands of the server or preparer, cooking equipment, or shared preparation surfaces.

The narrative continues with a series of paragraphs containing necessary background facts and all the legally relevant facts

Fun Zone is an entertainment establishment open to the public. It contains video and arcade games and serves a variety of food items and beverages. Hundreds of children have birthday parties every year at Fun Zone's five area locations. To have a party at Fun Zone, patrons must purchase a party package. All party packages include mandatory food and drink purchases (in specified minimum amounts) for each party guest, and that food and drink minimum is included in the party package price.

The paragraphs use clear topic sentences and flow logically; the important facts are described with specifics rather than generalities

Elaine wanted to have her eighth birthday party at Fun Zone. But because of the number and severity of her allergies, Elaine cannot safely eat any of Fun Zone's food. Almost every item on the menu contains at least one ingredient Elaine is allergic to. The other items might come in contact with a trace amount of her allergens in Fun Zone's kitchen, so she cannot safely eat those foods either. To accommodate her allergies, Elaine's mother requested that Fun Zone make an exception to its outside food policy and allow her to bring in all the food and drinks for her party. This would

The tone remains objective and avoids dramatic language; the writer includes only facts, not legal conclusions or opinions

allow Elaine to have a party like any other person's, where she could eat the same party food as all the other children.

Fun Zone refused Elaine's request. Fun Zone said it would allow Elaine to bring in food for herself and would waive the mandatory purchase fee for Elaine's food and drink, but it would not allow her to bring in food for any of the other party guests. An average of half of Fun Zone's profit from each birthday party comes from food and drink purchases. And birthday guests typically purchase more than the minimum food and drink requirement. Fun Zone's waitstaff are usually tipped based on the total food and drink bill. Fun Zone said providing food and drink was integral to its party packages, and it worried about the precedent it would set for changing its policy against outside food to accommodate an entire birthday party. Fun Zone thus would not make all the requested changes, and Elaine could not have her party there.

The section ends by framing the current issue

V.   Discussion

*The **Conclusion** briefly answers the question and gives a basis for the predicted outcome*

Elaine's request for Fun Zone to modify its policy prohibiting outside food to accommodate her food allergy was likely reasonable, considering the need to keep Elaine safe while allowing her a typical party experience and the minimal burden on Fun Zone to grant her the accommodation. The Americans with Disabilities Act (ADA) prohibits a place of public accommodation from discriminating based on disability. *See* 42 U.S.C. § 12182(a). One type of discrimination occurs if a place of public accommodation fails "to make reasonable modifications in policies, practices, or procedures" unless those modifications would "fundamentally alter" the nature of the business. *Id.* § 12182(b)(2)(A)(ii). It is undisputed that Fun Zone is a place of public accommodation subject to the Act and that Elaine's food allergies constitute a disability. Thus, the only issue analyzed is whether Elaine's request was reasonable.

*The **Rule** uses the highest authority first and moves from broad to narrow*

*The **Explanation** helps the reader further understand the rule and see how it applied in particular situations*

The plaintiff has the burden of showing that her requested modification was reasonable. *Johnson v. Gambrinus Co./ Spoetzl Brewery*, 116 F.3d 1052, 1058 (5th Cir. 1997); *Vorhees v. Pizza Place, Inc.*, 393 F. Supp. 3d 203, 212 (S.D. Tex. 2018). A request is reasonable if it is "reasonable in the general sense, that is, reasonable in the run of cases." *Johnson*, 116 F.3d at 1059; *see also US Airways, Inc. v. Barnett*, 535 U.S.

391, 401 (2002) (discussing ADA reasonable accommodations in the employment context as being "reasonable on [their] face, *i.e.*, ordinarily or in the run of cases"). This should be evaluated flexibly, on a case-by-case basis, focusing on factors such as the nature of the disability and the cost involved. *See Vorhees*, 393 F. Supp. 3d at 212.

The reasonableness of a requested modification is distinct from whether the modification would fundamentally alter the nature of the business. *See Johnson*, 116 F.3d at 1059–60. The reasonable modification inquiry focuses on "the general nature of the accommodation" while the fundamental alteration defense examines "the specifics of the plaintiff's or defendant's circumstances." *Id.* at 1060. Fundamental alteration is an affirmative defense that the defendant must plead and prove. *See id.* at 1059 ("If the plaintiff meets this burden [of showing she requested a reasonable modification], the defendant must make the requested modification unless the defendant pleads and meets its burden of proving that the requested modification would fundamentally alter the nature of the public accommodation.").

A case illustration shows how the rule applied under particular circumstances; it begins with a topic sentence that gives the outcome on the issue and a few determinative facts; it provides the court's reasoning and holding

In *Vorhees*, a dairy-allergic man's request to bring his own meal into a pizza restaurant was deemed facially reasonable. 393 F. Supp. 3d at 212. The customer wanted to accompany his family for a meal at the pizza restaurant, but because of his severe dairy allergy, he could not eat the restaurant's food without risking death from an allergic reaction. *See id.* at 211. The restaurant had a nationwide policy prohibiting customers from bringing their own food. *Id.* The customer asked the restaurant to make an exception to accommodate his disability, but the restaurant refused, claiming it would have to assess the validity of every customer's claimed food allergy, which would be unreasonable as a matter of law. *See id.* at 212. The court denied the company's motion to dismiss, reasoning that a modification allowing the customer to eat with his family at the restaurant without risking a potentially fatal allergic reaction was facially reasonable in the run of cases, even if a customer might in some instances attempt to fake a food allergy. *See id.* The court emphasized that the plaintiff had not requested that the restaurant prepare safe food for him or take any other affirmative actions to accommodate him, which further demonstrated the general reasonableness of the customer's request. *See id.*

Similarly, Elaine's request for Fun Zone to modify its policies and allow her to bring in her own party food was likely reasonable. It is undisputed that Elaine, like the customer in *Vorhees*, cannot safely eat any of Fun Zone's food without risking a potentially fatal allergic reaction. *Id.* at 211. Both Fun Zone and the company in *Vorhees* initially refused to allow their food-allergic customers to bring in safe food, even though that would not have required the companies to alter their cooking procedures or attempt to provide the customers a safe meal. *See id.* at 212; *see also J.D. v. Colonial Williamsburg Found.*, 925 F.3d 663, 675 (4th Cir. 2019) (considering, in evaluating the reasonableness of gluten-sensitive plaintiff's request to bring in his own food, whether the defendant would be required "to take any action or provide any additional services").

Under the reasoning in *Vorhees*, Elaine's request, which would allow her to enjoy a party at Fun Zone without risking death, should be deemed facially reasonable. *See Vorhees*, 393 F. Supp. 3d at 212. Moreover, Elaine would still pay Fun Zone for using its facility, only requiring that Fun Zone step back and let Elaine ensure her own safety while allowing her to fit in with her friends by sharing common food. Thus, a request to modify Fun Zone's policies to allow Elaine to keep herself safe while enjoying a typical party experience is likely reasonable in the run of cases. *See id.*; *see also Barnett*, 535 U.S. at 401; *Johnson*, 116 F.3d at 1059.

Fun Zone will likely make two arguments to the contrary. First, Fun Zone will say it acted reasonably because it offered to allow Elaine to bring in food for herself even if not for her guests. Since Elaine is the one with the food allergy, outside food is unnecessary to keep the other children safe, and losing revenue only from Elaine's share of the food would be minimal. Yet enacting Fun Zone's proposal would deprive Elaine of the experience of sharing food, particularly a birthday treat such as a cake, with her party guests. Moreover, even if Fun Zone's option were reasonable, that misses the point. The statute says that a plaintiff must offer a reasonable modification, *see* 42 U.S.C. § 12182(b)(2)(A)(ii), and the defendant counter-proposing a different rea-

---

The **Application** begins with a clear shift to the client's case and a broad thesis that states the issue's outcome

The application continues, using specific facts and comparisons to precedent to make the argument

The **Counterargument** makes a clear shift to the opposing argument

The counterarguments are presented specifically and rebutted directly, and the transition between the parts is clear

sonable option does not render the plaintiff's option unreasonable.

Second, Fun Zone will likely argue that forcing it to allow anyone with a food allergy or other food-restricting condition to have a birthday party without the revenue from food and beverage sales would undermine its business model and be much too costly. This argument, which focuses specifically on the defendant's individual circumstances, relates to the affirmative defense of fundamental alteration, not the plaintiff's burden to show her requested modification was generally reasonable. *See Johnson*, 116 F.3d at 1059–60. Fun Zone has thus far not pleaded any affirmative defenses, and unless it amends its pleadings to include the fundamental alteration affirmative defense, it will be precluded from making any such individualized argument. *See Riel v. Elec. Data Sys. Corp.*, 99 F.3d 678, 684 (5th Cir. 1996) (limiting inquiry in ADA employment case to the reasonableness of an accommodation request because the defendant did not plead undue burden affirmative defense); *see also Johnson*, 116 F.3d at 1058–59 (applying the *Riel* burdens and framework in the public accommodations context).

The **Conclusion** states the outcome and briefly gives the basis for it

Elaine's request that Fun Zone modify its policy against outside food would have allowed her to safely enjoy a birthday party experience like that of any other child and would at most minimally burden Fun Zone. Thus, her request was likely reasonable in the run of cases.

VI. Conclusion

Because Elaine's request for Fun Zone to modify its restriction on outside food did not require additional work on Fun Zone's part and would have allowed Elaine to enjoy a typical birthday party experience, her request was likely reasonable. Given your instructions for this memo and Fun Zone's pleading deficiency, I analyzed only the reasonableness of the proposed modification and not the fundamental alteration defense. If you anticipate that Fun Zone might amend its pleadings to assert a fundamental alteration defense and would like for me to conduct further research and analysis on that issue or any other, please let me know.

The Memo's Conclusion states the outcome and basis, and then it gives a specific suggestion for potential follow-up

MEMORANDUM

TO: Partner

FROM: Associate

DATE: September 17, 2020

RE: Ward's Bystander and Respondeat
         Superior Claims Against Grant Coulson and
         Home Shield, Inc. (file 001953.0201)

The **Heading** contains the recipient, author, current date, and a brief statement of the specific issue; it is aligned and has ample white space

I. Introduction

The **Introduction** sets out the client, the specific issue, a reference to the rule, the conclusion, and the basis for the conclusion

Our client, Melinda Ward has sued Grant Coulson and Home Shield, Inc., for negligent infliction of emotional distress based on a bystander theory. Coulson's vehicle struck Ward's son, Leo, in the parking lot of an office supply store. Ward was standing near the accident and claims bystander injuries for the shock of her experience. The claim against Home Shield stems from respondeat superior; Coulson was buying office supplies for his supervisor at the time of the accident. This memo addresses two issues: (1) the contemporaneous and sensory perception element of a bystander claim and (2) the course and scope of employment issue of a respondeat superior claim. Ward probably cannot establish the contemporaneous and sensory perception element because she did not realize her son had been in an accident until after it had happened. Ward probably cannot establish the respondeat superior claim against Home Shield because Coulson was acting against his employer's direction when he drove to an office supply store to buy supplies in person.

II. Questions Presented

A.   Under Texas bystander law, which requires a contemporaneous and sensory perception of a traumatic event, did Ward contemporaneously perceive the car accident when she heard a vehicle hit her son but only realized what had happened after the driver cried out and she turned to see the aftermath?

B.   Under Texas respondeat superior law, which subjects an employer to liability for acts of its employees in the course and scope of their employment, was Coulson acting in the course and scope of his employment when he was buying office supplies for his supervisor at the time of the

The **Questions Presented** both follow the same accepted format, raise the precise question, and give the legal context with some specific facts; they are readable and concise

accident, but his supervisor had specifically told him to obtain the supplies a different way?

III.   Brief Answers

A.   Ward probably cannot establish the contemporaneous and sensory perception element of a bystander claim because she learned that her son had been injured after the accident happened. To establish the contemporaneous and sensory perception element, a plaintiff must experience a loved one's accident at the same time it happens. Ward did not see Coulson's car hit her son, and Coulson cried out after the accident. Only then did Ward realize that the thumping sound she heard earlier was a car accident, after which she turned to see her son. This delayed reaction is not contemporaneous and therefore is probably insufficient for a bystander claim.

B.   Ward probably cannot establish a respondeat superior claim against Home Shield because Coulson took it upon himself to obtain supplies in an unauthorized manner and thus was not acting in the course and scope of his employment when the accident happened. An employee is on a special mission for an employer—and is thus acting in the course and scope of employment—if the task is in furtherance of the employer's business and with the employer's express or implied permission. Coulson's duties included purchasing office supplies for his supervisor, but he was told to order them using an emailed form. Although he had driven his car to buy supplies in person a few times before, he was not authorized to do so. Coulson probably was not on a special mission when the accident happened.

IV.   Statement of Facts

Melinda Ward has sued Grant Coulson as a bystander based on a parking-lot accident in which Coulson's SUV struck her son Leo, leaving Leo with brain damage. Ward asserts that Coulson's employer, Home Shield, is responsible for the accident because Coulson is Home Shield's employee and was buying office supplies for his supervisor at the time of the accident.

Coulson is an administrative assistant at Home Shield, where he works for owner Jemma Johnson. Coulson described his duties as "whatever Ms. Johnson needs me to [do]." He is supposed to "make her life easier and help her

*The **Brief Answers** quickly answer the questions, echo the question language, and follow the Conclusion-Rule-Application-Conclusion format*

The questions presented and brief answers work together to give the reader a concise, standalone overview of the key facts, law, and analysis

*The **Statement of Facts** begins by orienting the reader to the parties and current issue*

do her job as well as possible." Within that broad directive, Coulson has specifically assigned duties, such as monitoring and restocking the company's office supplies and ordering special supplies when needed. Johnson requires Coulson to order supplies from Simmons Office Supply, a local business she likes to support. To place an order, Coulson must fill out a paper form, scan the form, and email it to Simmons. Once an order is placed, the supply store takes about one week to deliver the supplies.

The narrative continues with a series of paragraphs containing necessary background facts, all legally relevant facts, and any pertinent emotional facts

Coulson views the email ordering process as cumbersome, and he tries to circumvent it when possible. Three or four times before the day of the accident, Coulson had obtained supplies by visiting the store in person rather than by using the email ordering process. The first time Coulson shopped that way, he was late to the office because the supply store opened at 8:00 a.m., the same time Coulson was supposed to start work. Johnson "busted" Coulson for being late. Other than chiding him for his lateness, Johnson did not discourage Coulson from ordering supplies in person but simply raised her eyebrow and walked off. Johnson knew about other instances when Coulson shopped in person for supplies and was then late to work; she did not correct him then either because she wanted to "cut him some slack" due to his personal problems with his wife. It is undisputed, though, that Coulson was supposed to be in the office during his working hours, which start at 8:00 a.m., and that Johnson had directed Coulson to use the paper ordering process for office supplies.

On the day of the accident, Coulson was picking up supplies from Simmons in person rather than using the email ordering process. Johnson had a presentation at 9:00 a.m. that day, and she needed several colors of dry erase markers for that purpose. Coulson had forgotten to order the markers when she asked him to do so three weeks earlier, so he went to the store in person to ensure Johnson would have them in time for the presentation. As he drove into the parking lot, Coulson was texting and speeding, and he did not see Leo in his path.

The paragraphs use clear topic sentences and flow logically; the important facts are described with specifics rather than generalities

The tone remains objective and avoids dramatic language; the writer includes only facts, not legal conclusions or opinions

At the same time, Ward too was in the Simmons parking lot after buying supplies. As she strapped her baby into her car seat, her son Leo was standing at her side. As Ward took a few moments to buckle up the car seat straps, she did not see where Leo was. Ward then heard a sound she described as a "strange thumping sound," but Ward did not know what it was. A few seconds later, she heard a car door open and a man said, "Oh no, what have I done?" As soon as she heard these words, Ward realized that Leo was not beside her, and she knew that the sound meant he had been hit. Ward did not see the accident, but she turned around and saw Leo unconscious on the ground in front of a large SUV.

Ward then screamed for the man to call 911, which he did. An ambulance arrived quickly, and then paramedics stabilized Leo and drove him and Ward to the hospital. Leo suffered permanent brain damage and is unable to walk. Ward claims damages for weight loss, headaches, nightmares, and other physical symptoms resulting from the shock of her experience of the accident. Ward sued Coulson and Home Shield in Texas state court in Houston, claiming damages as a bystander and that Home Shield is liable for Coulson's conduct based on respondeat superior.

The section ends by framing the current issue

V. Discussion

Ward probably cannot establish the contemporaneous and sensory perception element of her bystander claim because she did not realize the accident had happened until after the fact. Ward probably cannot establish a respondeat superior claim against Home Shield because Coulson took it upon himself to buy supplies in an unauthorized manner and thus was not on a special mission for his employer when the accident happened.

*The **Roadmap** states both conclusions and briefly states the basis for each; because the two issues here have different overall rules, the overall rules are stated within each section rather than within the roadmap*

A. Ward learned her son was injured only after the accident was over, so she did not contemporaneously experience the accident.

*The **Conclusion** briefly answers the question and gives a basis for the predicted outcome*

Ward probably cannot establish a bystander claim because she did not see her son's accident and only realized her son was hurt after the accident took place. To recover as a bystander, a plaintiff (1) must be near the accident, rather than a distance away; (2) must suffer shock as a result of a direct emotional impact from a "sensory and contemporaneous observance" of the accident, rather than learning about it from another; and (3) must be closely related to the victim. *United Servs. Auto. Ass'n v. Keith*, 970 S.W.2d 540, 542 (Tex. 1998). Because Ward was only feet away from the accident and she is obviously closely related to her son, the

The writer briefly states the overall rule and explains why some elements are not discussed

distance and close-relationship elements will be met. This memo thus addresses only the sensory and contemporaneous observance element.

The sensory and contemporaneous observance element requires that a plaintiff perceive a loved one's catastrophic accident at the same time the accident happens. *Id.* If a plaintiff comes upon the scene after being notified of the accident, this element generally is not satisfied. *Id.* Bystander recovery is meant to compensate a narrow and specific harm: the sudden and horrific observation of a loved one's injury or death. *See Chapa v. Traciers & Assocs.*, 267 S.W.3d 386, 398 (Tex. App. 2008) (affirming summary judgment for the defendant where the mother did not see her car towed away with her children inside and the children were in fact unharmed).

A mother did not establish the sensory and contemporary observance element, for example, when she was informed at home that something had happened to her daughter, and she then immediately rushed to the car accident scene. *Keith*, 970 S.W.2d at 542. The mother arrived in time to see her daughter's car still smoking and a tail light blinking; her daughter was suffering at the scene. *Id.* at 541. Even so, the mother did not establish the sensory and contemporaneous observance element because she witnessed the immediate aftermath of the accident rather than the accident itself. *Id.* The Texas Supreme Court emphasized that both presence at the scene and "contemporaneous perception of the accident" are required to recover. *Id.*

A Texas appellate court outside Houston, where this case was filed, allowed recovery in narrower circumstances, when a plaintiff arrived at the scene right after an accident. *See City of Austin v. Davis*, 693 S.W.2d 31, 34 (Tex. App. 1985). In *City of Austin*, the court permitted recovery because the father was directly involved in the search for his son, which ended with the father's finding him deceased at the bottom of a ten-story air shaft. *Id.* at 33. The father was "intensely involved" in the search and was "brought so close to the reality of the accident as to render [his] experience an integral part of it." *Id.* at 34.

Here, Ward probably cannot establish the contemporaneous sensory observance element because when she heard

---

The Rule uses the highest authority first and moves from broad to narrow

A case illustration shows how the rule applied under particular circumstances; it begins with a topic sentence that gives the outcome on the issue and a few determinative facts; it provides the court's reasoning and holding

The **Explanation** helps the reader further understand the rule and see how it applied in particular situations

The explanation further describes how another court applied the rule in particular circumstances

the car hitting her son, she did not know the sound's significance. And when Ward turned to see the accident's aftermath, she had been alerted to what had happened, so she did not come unwittingly upon the scene.

While she was buckling her other child into a car seat, Ward lost track of her son; although Ward heard the sound of a car hitting him, she did not know what the sound was, so she cannot satisfy the contemporaneous and sensory observance requirement. Texas courts insist that a bystander plaintiff's perception of the accident be contemporaneous, so that the recovery compensates the plaintiff's experience of "actually witnessing the realization of such fears firsthand." *Chapa*, 267 S.W.3d at 399. When she heard the accident, Ward did not know what was happening, so that portion of her experience does not permit recovery.

Moreover, when Ward turned and saw the accident's aftermath (her son lying unconscious on the pavement), she did not come upon the scene unwittingly. Coulson's cry of "What have I done?" had alerted Ward that her son was nowhere to be seen and that the sound she had just heard was the sound of a vehicle hitting him. Ward's experience was thus akin to that of the mother in *Keith*, who did not satisfy the contemporaneous and sensory observance element because she learned about the car accident before she arrived on the scene and saw her daughter suffering. *See Keith*, 970 S.W.2d at 541. Ward therefore probably cannot establish the contemporaneous and sensory experience element because her shock did not come from perceiving the accident when it occurred.

On the other hand, it could be argued that although Ward did not realize what was happening when she heard the accident, she was so involved in the accident and the events unfolded so fast that her experience was more akin to those who were "brought so close" to the experience of the accident that they satisfied the contemporaneous and sensory experience element. *See City of Austin*, 693 S.W.2d at 34. Although Ward did not immediately recognize the "thud" as the sound of a vehicle hitting her son, she quickly realized what had happened. She experienced the accident with her senses when it occurred, even if the dreadful realization followed seconds later. Arguably, Ward was so involved in the accident that her experience was similar to that

---

The margin notes:

The **Application** begins with a clear shift to the client's case and includes a broad thesis that states the issue's outcome

The paragraphs contain transition words and strong topic sentences so that the reader understands the argument's structure

The application continues, using specific facts from the client's case and comparing them to explicit facts from precedent cases that were discussed above; the writer then gives the inference to be drawn from the comparison

The **Counterargument** makes a clear shift to the opposing argument

The counter-argument is presented specifically and rebutted directly, and the transition between counter-argument and rebuttal is clear

of the father in *City of Austin*, who recovered even though he came upon his son after the accident and did not see his son's fall into the air shaft. *Id.*

This argument should fail for two reasons. First, *City of Austin* is not binding on our court, both because it was issued from an appellate court outside our jurisdiction and because it is inconsistent with the Texas Supreme Court's more recent opinion in *Keith*. In *Keith*, the Texas Supreme Court reiterated the requirement that the shock of the sensory perception occur at the same time as the accident. *Keith*, 970 S.W.2d at 542. Ward's shock was due not to the accident but its aftermath. Ward stated that she felt dread and shock when she heard Coulson cry out, which was after the accident's impact. Second, Ward's experience was different from the father's in *City of Austin* because Coulson's cry warned Ward of a terrible event, whereas the father had no warning but knew only that his son was missing. *See City of Austin*, 693 S.W.2d at 34.

Ward probably cannot establish the contemporaneous and sensory observance element of a bystander claim because her shock resulted from the aftermath of her son's accident rather than the contemporaneous perception itself.

B. Ward probably cannot establish a respondeat superior claim against Home Shield because Coulson's vehicle struck Leo while Coulson was buying office supplies in person without authorization.

Because Coulson was shopping in person without authorization at the time of the accident, Ward probably cannot establish that Coulson was acting in the course and scope of his employment. For an employer to be liable for an employee's negligence, the employee's acts must be within the course and scope of the employment. *Painter v. Amerimex Drilling I, Ltd.*, 561 S.W.3d 125, 131 (Tex. 2018). An act is within the course and scope of employment if it falls under the employee's general authority and is to further the employer's business. *Id.* at 136. An employer is generally not liable for an employee's negligence on the way to and from work. *Id.* An exception to this rule exists for employees who undertake a "special mission at the direction of [the] employer" or who otherwise perform a service "in furtherance of [the] employer's business with the express or implied consent of [the] employer." *Id.* The employer's direction may be express or implied. *See Soto v. Seven Seventeen HBE Corp.*, 52 S.W.3d 201, 205–06 (Tex. App. 2000). Implied authorization may be created through the employee's repetition of the action, with the employer's knowledge and assent. *Id.* at 205.

The Explanation further shows how other courts have applied the rule and how particular circumstances have affected the outcome

An employee is not on a special mission where the employee takes it upon himself to perform a task in a way that the employer neither desired nor requested. *See id.* at 207. When, for example, a hotel employee accidentally took some keys home but then returned the keys that day, the employee was not on a special mission during the return trip. *Id.* The employer neither anticipated that employees would return keys right away nor disciplined employees who retained keys, and thus the employee's supervisor "would neither expect nor require" an employee to return to work just to bring back the keys. *Id.* Likewise, there was no special mission when an employee's job duties included reading work-related paperwork, but the duties did not extend to reading the paperwork on her lap while driving. *Garza v. Well Med Med. Mgmt.*, 35 S.W.3d 45, 57 (Tex. App. 2000).

These short case explanations show how the rule applied in particular circumstances without the need for a full case illustration, which in this instance would provide unnecessary detail

An employee is on a special mission, on the other hand, if the employee is impliedly or directly asked to perform a task, even if the task is not normally part of the employee's duties. *Arbelaez v. Just Brakes Corp.*, 149 S.W.3d 717, 722 (Tex. App. 2004). A brake technician's breakfast run was potentially within the course and scope of employment, for example, where his manager had directly requested the breakfast. *Id.* at 723. The trip was at least partially to further the employer's ends. *Id.* The court therefore reversed summary judgment for the defendant employer. *Id.* at 724.

The **Application** begins with a clear shift to the client's case and a broad thesis that states the issue's outcome

Here, Coulson was not on a special mission for his employer at the time of the accident because he was supposed to order office supplies by email from his workplace, not buy them in person, and he was supposed to be in the office at that time. Thus, the trip to buy office supplies was not at his employer's direction and was not with his employer's express or implied consent.

Johnson, Coulson's supervisor, never asked him to buy office supplies in person on his way to work—in fact, she required the opposite. Johnson had set out a specific way that Coulson was supposed to buy office supplies, which was by emailing a supply order form to Simmons and then awaiting delivery of the supplies. In stopping at the supply store on his way to work, Coulson was acting in an unauthorized manner, just like the hotel employee in *Soto*. Coulson's employer never expected or asked him to pick up supplies in person, just as the supervisor in *Soto* never asked the hotel employee to make a special trip back to the hotel to return the keys. *See* 52 S.W.3d at 207. In *Soto*, there was no special mission because there was no policy or requirement that the employee return the keys in the manner he chose to do so. *Id.* Here, equally, Coulson's in-person supply purchase was not set out in any procedure, nor was there any indication that he would have been disciplined for not buying supplies that way. In fact, the in-person purchase required him to be late to work because Simmons did not open until 8:00 a.m., and Coulson was supposed to be at work by then. Johnson had even "busted" him for failing to purchase office supplies by email in the past. Because in-person purchasing was not within Coulson's duties, Coulson was not on a special mission.

Ward could argue, however, that Johnson's reaction to Coulson's past in-person ordering of office supplies created sufficient doubt to support implied authorization. In fact, Johnson admitted that although she did not approve of Coulson's in-person ordering of office supplies, she did not chastise him either because he was going through a difficult time with his wife. Instead, she simply raised an eyebrow at the Simmons shopping bags and said nothing. Thus, Johnson's actions arguably created implied authority. This argument will likely fail. While implied consent can follow repetition and assent, *see id.* at 205–06, a raised eyebrow is probably insufficient to create assent. If a mere facial movement were enough to create implied authority, claims of respondeat superior could proliferate based simply on perceptions of supervisors' facial expressions and mood. Liability generally hinges on more concrete evidence.

Thus, Coulson's trip to Simmons was probably not a special mission because he was shopping without his employer's authorization at the time the accident happened.

VI.   Conclusion

Ward likely cannot establish the contemporaneous and sensory perception element of her bystander claim because she did not realize her son had been in an accident until after the impact. Ward probably cannot establish the respondeat superior claim against Home Shield because Coulson was acting against his employer's direction when he drove to Simmons to buy the supplies.

Chapter 9

Sample Answers (with Annotations) to Even-Numbered Exercises

Answer to Exercise 2

The most effective choice is bolded; comments on each one's effectiveness are set out below.

Headings:

(1)

> TO: Lee Freedman
> FROM: Valena Litman
> REGARDING: Negligence

Comment: This heading is ineffective because it is not aligned, there is no white space between the lines, the date of the memo is missing, and the subject line does not include the case identifier or client's name and does not identify the specific subject of the memo.

(2)

TO:	Lee Freedman
FROM:	Valena Litman
DATE:	September 2, 2020
RE:	006945.004, Big K Groceries, Proximate Cause and Damages for Slip and Fall Negligence Claim

Comment: This heading is effective. It is aligned and includes white space and is thus easier to read. It includes the date and identifies the client, the case identifier, and the specific issues being analyzed.

(3)

FROM:	Valena Litman
TO:	Lee Freedman
DATE:	9/2/20
RE:	006945.004, Big K's Negligence Claim

Comment: This heading has several problems. First, the To and From fields are in the wrong order (To should be first). Second, the date should be written in full, spelling out the month and followed by the date and full year. Finally, the subject line is not specific enough.

Introductions:

(1) Leah Beety sued our client, Big K Groceries, for negligence after she slipped and fell in a puddle of spilled coffee in one of Big K's stores. This claim will likely fail for two reasons. First, Big K likely did not breach any duty because it had recently cleaned the floor. Second, an earlier car accident, not the fall, likely caused Beety's damages.

Comment: This introduction is effective because it is short, identifies the parties and client, gives a basic factual context, and specifies what the memo will discuss without going into much detail. It also provides the basic reasoning for the conclusions.

(2) Beety's negligence claim against Big K Groceries will fail. The elements of negligence are duty, breach of duty, causation, and damages. Liability flows from conduct that causes reasonably foreseeable harm. A harm is foreseeable if a person of ordinary intelligence should have reasonably anticipated the danger. Beety slipped in a puddle of coffee that, according to video footage, had been on the floor for under one minute. Big K had cleaned the floor five minutes earlier. It is not foreseeable that failing to monitor the floor for one minute would cause someone to fall. Moreover, Beety's damages are based on a back injury, but a car accident two months before the fall caused her back problems, not the fall.

Comment: This introduction is ineffective because it is much too long and detailed. The introduction should identify the parties and client and give the basic factual context without providing too many details, which will come in the next sections (question presented, brief answer, and statement of facts). Further, the prediction language is much too strong—it seems to guarantee an outcome, which is virtually always inappropriate.

Answer to Exercise 4

Part A: Question Presented

The most effective question presented is bolded; comments on each one's effectiveness are set out below.

(1) A parent's rights can be terminated if, among other things, termination would be in the child's best interest. Sara Ramada shares an affectionate relationship with her child, earned high scores in her parenting classes, and remedied the messy state of her apartment. Can Sara Ramada's parental rights to J.M. be terminated?

Comment: This question presented is effective in that it follows an accepted format (multi-sentence) and contains appropriate legal context, a specific legal question, and determinative and specific facts. It is ineffective, however, in two respects. First, it slants the facts in Ramada's favor by omitting any negative facts. Second, it asks whether Ramada's rights can be terminated, rather than whether termination would be in the child's best interest. The call of the question was to focus on the best interest element, so the question should not address the broader issue.

(2) Whether termination is in the best interest of J.M., when J.M. has an affectionate relationship with her mother.

Comment: This question presented is effective in that it follows an accepted format (whether) and contains a specific legal question. The legal context is missing, however, and the facts are too thin and do not present an accurate picture of the controversy.

(3) **Under Texas law, would termination of Ramada's parental rights be in J.M.'s best interest, when Ramada shares an affectionate relationship with J.M., earned high scores in her parenting classes, and remedied the messy state of her apartment, but persisted in seeing a known drug user?**

Comment: This question presented is effective in that it follows an accepted format (under/does/when) and contains appropriate legal context, a specific legal question, and determinative and specific facts. The facts are selected to represent both sides of the issue.

Part B: Brief Answer

The most effective brief answer is bolded; comments on each one's effectiveness are set out below.

(1) Probably not. Before a parent's rights can be terminated, termination must be in the child's best interest. Courts determine the child's best interest using factors such as the child's desires, the child's needs, potential danger to the child, available helpful programs, housing stability, a parent's acts and omissions, and potential excuses for those acts and omissions. Thus, the court should not terminate Ramada's rights.

Comment: This brief answer is effective to the extent that it begins with a short answer, states a rule, and ends with a conclusion. The answer is, however, missing an application section. Without knowing how the rule is satisfied, the reader cannot understand the writer's basis for the outcome. Furthermore, the conclusion addresses a broader issue than the question presented. That is, the question is whether termination would be in the child's best interest, not how the larger termination issue would be resolved. The brief answer should confine itself to the question presented.

(2) Ramada was generally a good parent, and her child liked to see her. To terminate a parent's rights, termination must be in the child's best interest. Thus, the court should not terminate Ramada's rights.

Comment: This brief answer is ineffective because it does not follow the proper format (Conclusion-Rule-Application-Conclusion), contains almost no specific facts, and does not conclude with a focus on the specific question presented.

(3) **Probably not. To terminate a parent's rights, termination must be in the child's best interest. Courts determine the child's best interest using various factors, including the child's desires, the child's needs, potential danger to the child, available helpful programs, housing stability, a parent's acts and omissions, and potential excuses for those acts and omissions. Ramada kept her child safe, maintained appropriate housing, and has a positive relationship with her child. Due to her own mother's illness, Ramada left her child with someone who used drugs; Ramada continues to see this person. On balance, however, terminating Ramada's rights would not be in her child's best interest.**

Comment: This brief answer is effective because it follows an accepted format, starts with a short conclusion, states a rule, and uses specific facts in the subsequent application. The facts are selected to show how the rule applies to Ramada's specific situation, including both sides of the issue, and the conclusion is specific to the issue at hand.

Answer to Exercise 6

Part A: Question Presented

The best choices for each component are indicated below in bold:

I. "Under" (Legal Context) Component:

A. Under FRCP 18,

B. Under the federal venue rules,

> Both A and B are too vague and do not provide sufficient legal context

> **C** informs the reader of the basic venue rule

C. Under Federal Rule of Criminal Procedure 18, which requires prosecution of crimes in the district in which the offense was committed,

II. "Does" (Legal Question) Component:

> B is an acceptable choice, but not as good as A; B refers to prosecution instead of venue and refers to the court instead of the district, and thus A is more precise and concise

A. is venue proper in the Central District of California

> The legal question at issue is venue, so **A** is the best choice

B. can Grayson be prosecuted in the United States District Court for the Central District of California

C. can a Central District of California jury convict Grayson of theft

> The legal issue is proper venue, not whether the defendant can be convicted, so **C** is correct

III. "When" (Facts) Component:

> A omits the critical fact that the exact location of the crime is unknowable

A. when the plane landed in the Central District of California?

B. when the district in which the air crime was committed cannot be determined but the plane landed in the Central District of California?

> **B** provides the two critical facts: where the plane landed and that the location of the crime is unknowable

> C is too long, unfocused, and full of clauses; it provides too many details; it also is not objectively worded (referring to the theft as obvious)

C. when Ms. Grayson obviously stole Ms. Romero's wallet during the flight and so the wallet was stolen somewhere between New York, where the plane took off, and Los Angeles, where the plane landed, but no one knows exactly where?

Part B: Brief Answer

This chart shows which sentences should be used in the brief answer, sets out the correct order, and explains the choices:

SENTENCE	INCLUDE?	EXPLANATION
(6) Probably not.	Yes	This prediction shows a high level of confidence but does not guarantee a certain outcome, which would be inappropriate in almost all instances.
(1) The venue rule requires the United States to prosecute the defendant in the district in which the offense was committed.	Yes	This rule statement varies some language used in the question presented but correctly duplicates the critical rule language.
(5) The prosecution cannot prove which district the plane was flying over at the time of the theft.	Yes	This is the critical fact—the fact on which the analysis turns—and thus is appropriate to include in the brief answer.
(8) Thus, venue is probably not proper in the Central District of California because the prosecution cannot prove the crime was committed in that district.	Yes	This conclusion states the predicted outcome, echoes the certainty of the prediction from the short answer, and explains the basis for the prediction.
(2) The plane landed in the Central District of California, so venue is proper there.	No	Where the plane landed does not tie back to the rule language regarding where the crime was committed, and so this explanation is confusing.
(3) No.	No	This prediction is too certain and appears to guarantee a certain result.

(4) The venue rule requires that a crime be prosecuted in the district in which the offense was committed.	No	This language is virtually identical to the legal context portion of the question presented. Readers usually prefer some variation in non-essential language.
(7) Venue is improper in the Central District of California.	No	This statement is too certain and conclusory. It should match the level of certainty in the opening prediction and should explain the basis for the conclusion.
(9) The venue rule requires a crime to be prosecuted where it happened.	No	This rule statement contains too much variation from the key rule language.

This is the sample brief answer, with all sentences that should be included in the correct order.

> Probably not. The venue rule requires the United States to prosecute the defendant in the district in which the offense was committed. The prosecution cannot prove which district the plane was flying over at the time of the theft. Thus, venue is probably not proper in the Central District of California because the prosecution cannot prove the crime was committed in that district.

Answer to Exercise 8

Part A: Question Presented

One way of writing the question presented for each issue (in the requested format) is below. Notice that each one includes the legal context, the legal question, and specific facts. The questions presented are concise and include only the facts that are critical for that particular question. The components are presented in a logical order and can be understood without requiring the reader to read any other part of the memo first. The questions also use consistent language when referring to the claims and parties.

Note: The exercise asked you to write in two different formats for practice purposes, but in a multi-issue memo, all questions presented should be written in the same format.

1. Under California law for invasion of privacy based on intrusion on seclusion, which requires an intentional intrusion on private affairs, is the defendant's viewing the plaintiff through binoculars eating dinner and watching television in his home an intrusion on the plaintiff's private affairs?

2. Recovery under California law for invasion of privacy based on intrusion on seclusion requires a showing that the intrusion would be highly offensive to a reasonable person. The defendant used binoculars to watch the plaintiff in his home through a large, street-facing window with no curtains. Is that conduct highly offensive to a reasonable person?

Part B: Brief Answer

One way of writing the brief answers to the questions presented for each issue in Part A above is below. Notice that there is one answer for each question presented and that the answers are in the same order as the questions. As with the questions, the answers use consistent language when referring to the claims and parties, and they echo the language used in the questions. The answers begin with a short, direct answer, followed by an explanation in Conclusion-Rule-Application-Conclusion format.

1. Probably yes. Invasion of privacy based on intrusion on seclusion requires an intentional intrusion on the plaintiff's private affairs. Private affairs include subject matter that an individual has a right to keep private. The plaintiff probably has a right to keep private his ordinary household activities such as eating and watching television.

2.   Probably no. A plaintiff must show that the intrusion would be highly offensive to a reasonable person. An intrusion is not highly offensive to a reasonable person if the person's expectation of privacy is unreasonable under the circumstances. The defendant viewed the plaintiff through a large window, with no curtains, that faced the street. The plaintiff probably cannot reasonably expect privacy in whatever activities he conducts that can be seen through this window.

Answer to Exercise 10

This chart shows which sentences should be included and explains the choices, along with suggestions for revised language:

FACTS	INCLUDE?	RELEVANCE? APPROPRIATE LANGUAGE?
(1) Our client, Mary Jones, is a sweet lady of seventy-five, who alleges that she was improperly detained while shopping at Big Buy, an electronics store.	Yes, with revisions	All of these are important background facts that should be included. The description of Mary Jones as "sweet" is stereotypical and not objective and thus should not be included.
(2) Jones was shopping for a new iPhone case for her niece.	Partial	This background information about her shopping trip should be included, except for the gift's intended recipient, which does not bear on any issue in the case.
(3) As she was comparing two iPhone cases, one slipped off the shelf and fell into her handbag.	Yes	This fact explains why Jones was detained and thus should be included.
(4) When Jones paid for one iPhone case and tried to leave the store, the security alarms went off.	Yes	To understand how Jones's detention took place, the reader will need these facts.

(5) The store's tall and intimidating security guard grabbed Jones by the arm and pulled her into a windowless and prisonlike office near the front of the store.	Yes, with revisions	The description of the guard as "intimidating" seems to be the author's opinion. If Jones stated that she found the guard intimidating, the facts should say that instead. Similarly, "prisonlike" is an opinion—the author should delete the word and use factual information instead. Finally, the office's exact location is not relevant.
(6) Other shoppers gathered in a mob near the office.	Yes, with revisions	The gathering of shoppers is a relevant background fact for the detention's conditions, but the word "mob" is overly dramatic, given the lack of any facts to support the characterization.
(7) After what seemed like an eternity, but was actually twenty minutes, the guard released Jones.	Yes, with revisions	The detention's length is a legally significant fact, but the opinion that it "seemed like an eternity" is not attributed to anyone and appears to be the author's opinion. As such, it does not belong in the statement of facts.

Answer to Exercise 12

This chart shows the correct order for the sentences to create a chronological story with good flow and explains which dates are necessary and which are not:

SENTENCE	COMMENT
(1) Thelma and Louise were long-time friends.	This provides context for the actors' relationship.
(5) Thelma had always been a good driver before she turned sixty on May 1, 2019.	The exact date of her birthday is irrelevant.
(4) Thelma was declared legally blind in one eye on January 27, 2020, but Louise did not know this.	The exact date of her legal blindness does not matter. It is sufficient to establish legal blindness after her birthday but before the bakery incident.
(6) On March 28, 2020, Thelma drove up over the curb at her favorite bakery and into the bakery's front window when she mistook the gas pedal for the brake.	The date of the key incident showing Thelma's dangerous driving, of which Louise was aware, is significant.
(2) Thelma asked Louise to borrow Louise's car on April 1, 2020, because her own car was in the repair shop and she needed to run an errand.	The exact date she asked to borrow the car is unnecessary as long as the reader knows it was after the bakery incident.
(3) Louise knew that Thelma had crashed into the bakery's front window on March 28, 2020, because she had gotten confused about the pedals, but she let Thelma borrow the car anyway.	This date has already been established and doesn't need to be repeated.
(7) While driving Louise's car on April 1, 2020, Thelma hit a young boy riding a bicycle, severely injuring him.	The precise date does not matter as much as establishing that this occurred shortly after the bakery incident.

Here is the sample statement of facts with all sentences in the right order and with adjustments made to eliminate unnecessary dates and add other time-indicating phrases (marked in bold):

> Thelma and Louise were long-time friends. Thelma had always been a good driver before she turned sixty **last year**. Thelma was declared legally blind in one eye **this January**, but Louise did not know this. On March 28, 2020, Thelma drove up over the curb at her favorite bakery and into the bakery's front window when she mistook the gas pedal for the brake. Thelma asked Louise to borrow Louise's car **a few days later** because her own car was in the repair shop and she needed to run an errand. Louise knew that Thelma had crashed into the bakery's front window **earlier that week** because she had gotten confused about the pedals, but she let Thelma borrow the car anyway. While driving Louise's car **that day**, Thelma hit a young boy riding a bicycle, severely injuring him.

Answer to Exercise 14

The bolded choices are more effective than the non-bolded choices for the reasons described in the comment boxes.

Use the name and procedural term together initially, to clarify the parties and their names

[Plaintiff] or [**Plaintiff Alan White**] is suing [Defendant] or [**Defendant Charles Washington**] for negligence based on Washington's [grossly negligent acts] or [**actions**] or [careless acts] after White suffered a snake bite during a camping trip.

"Grossly negligent acts" is a legal conclusion that is not appropriate here; "careless" is an improper characterization

White, a twenty-year-old college student, was camping [with Mary White, Susan White, Lila White, and Bob White, his family members] or [**with his family**] or [with his dear family] in Big Bend National Park when a [**five-foot**] or [large] or [large and extremely intimidating] snake bit him. At the same time, Washington, a forty-year-old attorney, was hiking on a sandy trail with his family when he heard screams coming from the nearby bushes. The screams were from White, [**who had stepped on the snake**] or [who had unfortunately stepped on the snake]. The [beautiful yet threatening snake suddenly struck him] or [**snake struck him**] or [snake struck him savagely].

Avoid having your reader learn unnecessary names; avoid unnecessary descriptors such as "dear"

"Extremely intimidating" and "large" are both opinions

Avoid opinions such as "unfortunately"; "threatening" and "savagely" are also inappropriate opinions and are too dramatic

Washington ran over to White and tried to help. Washington had taken a first-aid class about thirty years earlier and thought he remembered how a snake bite should be treated. [Defendant] or [**Washington**] told White not to move a muscle, and Washington placed a tight tourniquet on White's leg. White immediately questioned whether a tourniquet was the right approach. White said, "I'm an Eagle Scout, and I know from my training that you should not place a tourniquet on a snake-bitten limb. Tourniquets can be very dangerous." Washington persisted, [recklessly tightening] or [**tightening**] or [stubbornly tightening] the tourniquet even further. After ten minutes, [Plaintiff] or [plaintiff] or [**White**] could not feel any sensation in his foot. White asked Washington again to remove the tourniquet; Washington [seemed very confident] or [**said he was "confident about the tourniquet"**] or [acted in good faith] and refused to remove it.

"Recklessly" is a legal term of art indicating a culpable mental state, so it should be avoided in a statement of facts; "stubbornly" is an opinion

Procedural terms are harder to follow than names; avoid using procedural terms alone

Here, it's best to use Washington's exact words to show his mental state; the other choices are an opinion ("seemed very confident") or a legal conclusion ("in good faith")

The tourniquet was so tight that it caused permanent injury. The snake bite itself caused no harm because the snake was nonvenomous and its teeth had barely grazed White's skin. [**White now claims that Washington's actions were grossly negligent.**] or [Washington's actions were probably grossly negligent.]

The statement of facts can state the plaintiff's claims, but it should not state a conclusion about that claim

Answer to Exercise 16

Step 1: Underline the Facts

The underlined facts should be included in a statement of facts for the reasons stated in the comment boxes.

> Susan Johnson lived in Miami, Florida, with her two children, and her beloved and gentle rescue terrier, Gizmo. As a hurricane approached, the dog would not fit in the car as they tried to evacuate.

Gizmo's temperament is not important to understand the facts or claims here

These are background facts; no need to state that Johnson loves her dog or that he was rescued (too dramatic)

> The hurricane gathered strength and continued on track toward Miami; Johnson struggled with her options. Johnson remembered a local shelter, the Pet Friends Emergency Pet Shelter, and she took Gizmo to the intake office. "I just need help until the hurricane passes," Johnson said. "OK," said the shelter manager. "We can take him. Just wait until at least two days after the hurricane to come and get him. Make sure you're back within fifteen days from now, or we will adopt him out. There's a $20 hurricane shelter fee for this."

The evacuation is important because it precipitated leaving Gizmo at the shelter

> "Please take care of him. Gizmo, baby, I love you. Be safe." The shelter manager looked at the form. "Looks good, she said. Johnson paid the $20 fee, kissed Gizmo on the nose, and watched as he was led away to the kennels. Johnson quickly returned to her apartment and continued to gather her belongings for the evacuation. She traveled two hundred miles north to a small hotel and waited with her children.

These details about Johnson's parting words and how she evacuated are not legally significant

Her travel 200 miles away helps explain the delay in attempting to retrieve Gizmo, but the additional detail is not needed

> The following day, the storm hit. Johnson's apartment was severely damaged. She looked online for an undamaged apartment, but there were few choices, especially for a larger dog like Gizmo. She called the Pet Friends shelter intending to update the staff on her situation, but the line was always busy.

This information explains why Johnson could not pick up her dog and is thus needed background information

> After the storm, the shelter's files became disorganized, and the regular file clerk quit due to her family's problems with the storm. Gizmo stayed at the shelter for a week after the storm, but then he became separated from his file, and the shelter manager decided he should be adopted out.

This information explains why Gizmo was adopted out prematurely and is thus needed background information

> At the same time Gizmo was adopted out, Johnson finally found an apartment willing to take the family and Gizmo too. She quickly learned, however, that Gizmo had been adopted by another family. She now wants to enforce the bailment agreement and to challenge the new adoption contract on the basis of mutual mistake.

This information brings the reader up to date and transitions to the next memo section

Step 2: Rewrite with Paragraphs

The statement of facts now begins with an orientation paragraph

Our client, Susan Johnson, claims that she entered into a bailment agreement with an animal shelter when she temporarily left her dog with a shelter during a hurricane; the shelter adopted the dog out to another family prematurely, during the post-storm chaos. Johnson now seeks to enforce her bailment agreement and have the new adoption agreement rescinded due to mutual mistake.

Facts describing Johnson's state of mind and other people's actions during the hurricane are omitted as non-essential

Johnson lived in Miami, Florida, with her two children and her terrier, Gizmo. As a hurricane approached, the dog would not fit in the car as they tried to evacuate. Johnson therefore took Gizmo to the intake office at the nearby Pet Friends Emergency Pet Shelter. The shelter manager agreed to take Gizmo and asked that Johnson wait at least two days after the hurricane to retrieve him. The manager requested the $20 hurricane shelter fee and noted, "Make sure you're back within fifteen days from now, or we will adopt him out."

Specific facts stating how Johnson and the shelter entered into an agreement are included

The essential facts explaining why Johnson could not pick up the dog are retained but are presented more succinctly

Johnson and her children then left the city for a hotel 200 miles away. When the storm hit the following day, Johnson's apartment sustained severe damage. Johnson looked for a new apartment but did not find one immediately, due to a shortage of undamaged apartments that would permit a dog of Gizmo's size. She called the Pet Friends shelter intending to update the shelter on her situation, but the line was always busy.

Key facts explain succinctly how Gizmo came to be adopted out

Gizmo stayed at the shelter for a week after the storm, but then he became separated from his file, and the shelter manager decided he should be adopted out.

At the same time Gizmo was adopted out, Johnson finally found an apartment willing to take the family and Gizmo too. She quickly learned, however, that Gizmo had been adopted by another family. She now wants to enforce the bailment agreement and to challenge the new adoption contract on the basis of mutual mistake.

A final sentence brings the reader up to date with the current claim

Answer to Exercise 18

Option B is the better version. Here are seven specific problems with Option A:

1. The introductory conclusion does not cover all points. It mentions course and scope but not the employee issue or the ultimate question of vicarious liability.

2. The legal context is missing. Before discussing vicarious liability, which is an exception to the general rule of non-liability for third party conduct, the general rule should be stated.

3. The subrules regarding employee status and course and scope of employment should not be included in a roadmap paragraph because those are specific to just those particular elements.

4. Citations are missing for the rules.

5. No explanation is given for why the third element regarding timing is not being addressed.

6. The order of the elements in the final sentence is in the wrong order. The memo will discuss the employment issue first, because that feeds into the discussion of course and scope, and so the roadmap paragraph should discuss them in the same order.

7. No final conclusion is given.

See the following notes showing why Option B is better:

The introductory conclusion covers both elements and the ultimate conclusion

Citations are included

The elements are discussed in the right order

Mr. Burger will probably not be vicariously liable for Hudson's assault on Parks; although Hudson was most likely Mr. Burger's employee, he was probably not acting in the course and scope of his employment when he assaulted Parks. Tort law generally imposes no liability on one person for another's conduct. *Wisenhouse v. Armendez*, 14 S.W.3d 200, 201 (Tex. App. 2000). An exception provides that employers can be vicariously liable for a worker's tort if the worker is (1) an employee, (2) acting in the course and scope of employment, (3) at the time of the tortious conduct. *Id.* Hudson was on shift working for Mr. Burger when he threw the milkshake blender at Parks, and thus the timing element is not an issue. This memo will therefore address whether Hudson was an employee at the time of the assault and, if so, whether he was

The general rule provides legal context

The timing element is disposed of quickly and thus need not be addressed further

continued

acting in the course and scope of his employment when he assaulted Parks. Hudson was most likely a Mr. Burger employee because Mr. Burger controlled all essential details of Hudson's work. Because Hudson acted out of anger and not to further Mr. Burger's business, however, Hudson was probably not acting in the course and scope of his employment, and thus Mr. Burger will probably not be vicariously liable for his conduct.

A final conclusion is included

Answer to Exercise 20

Here are five specific problems with the conclusions in the exercise:

1. The introductory conclusion is much too long and detailed. The final conclusion is too short and cursory. See below for an example of how to write a conclusion that strikes a balance.

2. The prediction language is inconsistent between the two conclusions. The strength of the prediction must be the same every time it is mentioned in the memo.

3. The language answering the question is inconsistent between the two conclusions. The introductory conclusion addresses admissibility of the evidence while the final conclusion addresses chain of custody.

4. The introductory conclusion did not answer the question asked. The memo was to address whether the State could sufficiently establish the chain of custody, not the broader question of admissibility of the blood sample. The blood sample could be inadmissible for reasons other than problems with the chain of custody.

5. Citations should not be included. These conclusions should be short and direct, not cluttered with citations. Citations will appear in the body of your analysis.

These are improved conclusions that fix the identified problems:

Introductory Conclusion: The State can likely establish the chain of custody as far as practicable because, even though the officer did not turn in the blood sample for two days, he took safeguards to ensure that no one had access to the sample and it showed no signs of tampering.

Prediction language is consistent

The correct question is answered

A reason for the prediction is provided

Final Conclusion: Because the officer took measures designed to prevent access to the sample and the sample showed no indications it was altered, the State can likely establish the chain of custody as far as practicable, even though the officer stored the blood sample in his trunk for two days.

Key information but not too many details are provided

A reason for the prediction is provided

Answer to Exercise 22

For Argument 1, Option B is the most useful because Option B focuses on the issue that is relevant to our client, which is whether a very short detention can amount to false imprisonment. While Option A contains correct law, it is not tailored to the situation at hand and is therefore a less useful choice than Option B. Options C and D focus more on detention by intimidation, which is not part of Argument 1.

For Argument 2, Option D is the most useful. Option D focuses on intimidation as the basis of a detention. Option C is also useful, but it contains a reference to words creating a fear of force, which is not part of Argument 2. Argument 2 focuses on fear of incarceration, so Option D is the better choice.

Option A

> False imprisonment is the unlawful detention of another, where the person is "deprived of his personal liberty." Ga. Code Ann. § 51-7-20. A detention may be physical, but can also arise out of words, gestures, or other actions that give rise to a reasonable belief that force will be used if the plaintiff does not submit. *Smith v. Wal-Mart Stores E., LP*, 765 S.E.2d 518, 522 (Ga. Ct. App. 2014). If the defendant's actions operate on the will of the plaintiff and result in a reasonable fear of "personal difficulty or personal injuries," then the person is considered detained. *Id.*

Option B

This version begins with a reference to the time issue, which is highly relevant to Argument 1

> False imprisonment is an unlawful detention of another, where the person is "deprived of his personal liberty" for any length of time. Ga. Code Ann. § 51-7-20. Even if a person is held for the briefest amount of time, the person's liberty is still at stake and the detention meets the statutory length of time requirement. *Taylor v. Madison Stores*, 785 S.E.2d 718, 720 (Ga. Ct. App. 2016).

Option C

False imprisonment is the unlawful detention of another, where the person is "deprived of his personal liberty." Ga. Code Ann. § 51-7-20. A detention may be physical but can also arise out of words, gestures, or other actions that give rise to a reasonable belief that force will be used if the plaintiff does not submit. *Smith v. Wal-Mart Stores E., LP*, 765 S.E.2d 518, 522 (Ga. Ct. App. 2014). If the defendant's actions operate on the will of the plaintiff and result in a reasonable fear of "personal difficulty or personal injuries," then the person is considered detained. *Id.* A person is detained if the person is made to believe that incarceration would result from departure, even if the person is physically able to leave. *Trevino v. Macie's Stores*, 830 S.E.2d 318, 320 (Ga. Ct. App. 2019).

Option D

False imprisonment is the unlawful detention of another, where the person is "deprived of his personal liberty." Ga. Code Ann. § 51-7-20. If the defendant's actions operate on the will of the plaintiff and result in a reasonable fear of "personal difficulty or personal injuries," then the person is considered detained. *Id.* A person is detained if the person is made to believe that incarceration would result from departure, even if the person is physically able to leave. *Trevino v. Macie's Stores*, 830 S.E.2d 318, 320 (Ga. Ct. App. 2019).

This rule focuses on a fear of "personal difficulty" and fear of incarceration in particular, which is directly relevant to Argument 2

Answer to Exercise 24

The rule and case illustration provided can be improved by drafting the rule from general to specific, removing unnecessary quotations, discussing precedent in past tense, and citing after each rule and case illustration sentence.

RULE SENTENCES	INCLUDE?	REASONING
(4) A physician-patient relationship can be based on a contract or on the physician's acts. *Tower v. Pythe*, 576 P.2d 43, 44 (Cal. 2017).	Yes	The rule starts with the broadest statement, so the reader can understand the context.
(3) No direct contact between the two is required, nor must the two deal directly with one another at all for the relationship to arise. *Id.* at 45.	Yes	The rule goes on to narrow the description.
(5) Where a physician is on call and is consulted for advice, a physician-patient relationship arises where the on-call physician takes affirmative actions toward the patient's treatment. *Id.*	Yes	This information is important to a reader's understanding of how a relationship arises.
(1) Affirmative acts toward treatment may include listening to symptoms, evaluating information, and contributing to the patient's treatment plan. *Id.*	Yes	The statement is useful because it explains how a physician could create a relationship with a patient.
(2) The physician in our case likely did not create a physician-patient relationship because she was on call, but she refused to see the patient and had no contract to treat him.	No	This is a useful statement for a different part of the memo, but it is a conclusion and thus does not belong in the rule.

EXPLANATION SENTENCES	INCLUDE?	REASONING
(3) An on-call cardiologist created a physician-patient relationship with a patient, for example, when the cardiologist listened to a patient's symptoms, said the patient was likely suffering from gastric symptoms, and advised no further treatment. *Id.* at 46.	Yes	This sentence gives the case's outcome and basis for the outcome.
(4) A patient had presented in the emergency room with crushing chest pain. *Id.* The treating physician telephoned an on-call cardiologist and described the symptoms. *Id.*	Yes	These relevant facts should be included.
(2) Based on the cardiologist's diagnosis—gastric rather than cardiac problems—the emergency room physician allowed the patient to leave. *Id.*	Yes	This sentence sets out further important facts.
(5) The patient was in fact suffering from a disabling heart attack. *Id.*	Yes	This sentence completes the factual background.
(1) The court held that a physician-patient relationship existed based on the cardiologist's listening to symptoms, his diagnosis of the condition, and his statement that no further treatment was needed. *Id.*	Yes	This holding from the precedent case should be included.
(6) The on-call physician says, "This patient has gastric problems, not cardiac problems. I think he should be allowed to leave the hospital now, without further treatment."	No	This information from a case is quoted too extensively, is improperly in present tense instead of past, and lacks a citation.

continued

The sentences are combined in the correct order below:

A physician-patient relationship can be based on a contract or on the physician's acts. *Tower v. Pythe*, 576 P.2d 43, 44 (Cal. 2017). No direct contact between the two is required, nor must the two deal directly with one another at all for the relationship to arise. *Id.* at 45. Where a physician is on call and is consulted for advice, a physician-patient relationship arises where the on-call physician takes affirmative actions toward the patient's treatment. *Id.* Affirmative acts toward treatment may include listening to symptoms, evaluating information, and contributing to the patient's treatment plan. *Id.*

An on-call cardiologist created a physician-patient relationship with a patient, for example, when the cardiologist listened to a patient's symptoms, said the patient was likely suffering from gastric symptoms, and advised no further treatment. *Id.* at 46. A patient had presented in the emergency room with crushing chest pain. *Id.* The treating physician telephoned an on-call cardiologist and described the symptoms. *Id.* Based on the cardiologist's diagnosis—gastric rather than cardiac problems—the emergency room physician allowed the patient to leave. *Id.* The patient was in fact suffering from a disabling heart attack. *Id.* The court held that a physician-patient relationship existed based on the cardiologist's listening to symptoms, his diagnosis of the condition, and his statement that no further treatment was needed. *Id.*

Answer to Exercise 26

Option B is the right choice here. The case details provided in Option A are unnecessary. The sentence introducing the examples states only that courts have applied that same rule in other contexts. The short parentheticals provided in Option B give that other context without the unnecessary detail.

Answer to Exercise 28

This chart shows which rules should be used, sets out the correct order, and explains the choices:

RULE	INCLUDE?	EXPLANATION
(3) Punitive damages are recoverable only when the harm results from fraud, malice, or gross negligence. Tex. Civ. Prac. & Rem. Code Ann. § 41.003(a).	Yes	This is the broadest statement of the punitive damages rule and should be the starting point for the paragraph.
(4) Malice must be proven by clear and convincing evidence. *Echostar Satellite L.L.C. v. Aguilar*, 394 S.W.3d 276, 292 (Tex. App. 2012).	Yes	The legal standard for proving malice is important to assessing the amount of evidence and thus should be included.
(1) Malice requires a specific intent to cause substantial injury or harm. Tex. Civ. Prac. & Rem. Code Ann. § 41.001(7).	Yes	Malice is the standard at issue in this case, so it must be included with the basic definition of malice.
(7) Specific intent means that the actor desires the consequences of her act or believes the consequences are substantially certain to result. *Seber v. Union Pac. R.R. Co.*, 350 S.W.3d 640, 654 (Tex. App. 2011).	Yes	Malice depends on specific intent, so defining specific intent is important.
(6) A defendant is not liable for punitive damages if she acted in good faith and without wrongful intention. *Coinmach Corp. v. Aspenwood Apartment Corp.*, 417 S.W.3d 909, 922 (Tex. 2013).	Yes	This subrule qualifies and limits the malice standard and is relevant to the case facts and thus should be included.
(2) The elements of fraud are a material misrepresentation, which was false, and which was either known to be false when made or was asserted without knowledge of its truth, which was intended to be acted upon, which was relied upon, and which caused injury. *Sears, Roebuck & Co. v. Meadows*, 877 S.W.2d 281, 282 (Tex. 1994).	No	The case concerns only punitive damages based on malice, not on fraud, so the elements of fraud are irrelevant.

(5) Malice must be proven by clear and convincing evidence. *Wilen v. Falkenstein*, 191 S.W.3d 791, 800 (Tex. App. 2006).	No	A more recent intermediate appellate court case already said this. A second cite to an older case from the same court is unnecessary.
(8) A defendant is not liable for punitive damages if she acted in good faith and without wrongful intention. *Wilen v. Falkenstein*, 191 S.W.3d 791, 800 (Tex. App. 2006).	No	A Texas Supreme Court case says the same thing and is also more recent, so there is no need to include this case too.

The appropriate sentences are combined in the correct order below:

> Punitive damages are recoverable only when the harm results from fraud, malice, or gross negligence. Tex. Civ. Prac. & Rem. Code Ann. § 41.003(a). Malice must be proven by clear and convincing evidence. *Echostar Satellite L.L.C. v. Aguilar*, 394 S.W.3d 276, 292 (Tex. App. 2012). Malice requires a specific intent to cause substantial injury or harm. Tex. Civ. Prac. & Rem. Code Ann. § 41.001(7). Specific intent means that the actor desires the consequences of her act or believes the consequences are substantially certain to result. *Seber v. Union Pac. R.R. Co.*, 350 S.W.3d 640, 654 (Tex. App. 2011). A defendant is not liable for punitive damages if she acted in good faith and without wrongful intention. *Coinmach Corp. v. Aspenwood Apartment Corp.*, 417 S.W.3d 909, 922 (Tex. 2013).

Answer to Exercise 30

Here are sample answers for each of the three writing tasks, with commentary:

A. Parenthetical

A defendant who fails to use lawful alternatives or who conceals the plaintiff's whereabouts cannot assert a necessity defense. *See Patrick v. Owens*, 398 N.W.2d 21, 28 (Minn. 1999) (concealing from police); *Fortenberry v. Graham*, 267 N.W.2d 643, 647 (Minn. 1979) (not attempting to use alternatives).

Two cases were combined into one synthesized subrule, and parentheticals show which part of the synthesized rule came from which case

B. Short explanation

A citation follows each sentence

Factual details about the circumstances of the detentions are irrelevant to the second element and thus are omitted

The acceptable length of confinement is not absolute but will vary with each case. *See Fortenberry v. Graham*, 267 N.W.2d 643, 647 (Minn. 1979). For instance, in *Fortenberry*, a five-day detention was too long as a matter of law when the deprogrammers did not try to turn the plaintiff over to the police or initiate civil commitment proceedings and thus did not avail themselves of available legal alternatives. *See id.* On the other hand, in *Patrick*, the court found a fact issue as to the reasonability of the detention when the deprogrammer held the plaintiff for only nine hours and let him go shortly after learning the police were searching for him. *See Patrick v. Owens*, 398 N.W.2d 21, 28 (Minn. 1999).

Past tense is used when describing the cases

C. Case illustration

An introductory sentence clearly tells the reader why this case is important

Factual details about the circumstances of the detention are irrelevant to the second element and thus are omitted

A failure to contact police or to initiate civil commitment proceedings during the confinement period, for example, can show the confinement length was unreasonable. In *Fortenberry*, the defendant deprogrammers abducted the plaintiff and held him for five days, four of which were business days. *Fortenberry v. Graham*, 267 N.W.2d 643, 647 (Minn. 1979). During this time, they did not attempt to have the plaintiff civilly committed under the state procedure or to contact the police for assistance. *Id.* The court held that five days' confinement was unreasonable as a matter of law because the deprogrammers did not even try to use these lawful available alternatives to protect the plaintiff. *See id.*

A citation follows each sentence

Past tense is used in the case illustration

The court's holding and reasoning are clearly explained

Answer to Exercise 32

This is an annotated sample answer, with new material in bold:

~~When assessing whether an invasion is offensive, courts require the intrusion to be "unjustified or unwarranted." *Vaughn v. Drennon*, 202 S.W.3d 308, 320 (Tex. App. 2006). There can be no intrusion on seclusion if the plaintiff consented to the defendant's conduct. *Farrington v. Sysco Food Servs.*, 865 S.W.2d 247, 253 (Tex. App. 1993).~~ Invasion of privacy based on intrusion on seclusion has two elements: (1) an intentional intrusion on another's solitude, seclusion, or private affairs or concerns, which (2) would be highly offensive to a reasonable person. *Valenzuela v. Aquino*, 853 S.W.2d 512, 513 (Tex. 1993). **When assessing whether an invasion is offensive, courts require the intrusion to be "unjustified or unwarranted."** ***Vaughn v. Drennon*****, 202 S.W.3d 308, 320 (Tex. App. 2006). There can be no intrusion on seclusion if the plaintiff consented to the defendant's conduct.** ***Farrington v. Sysco Food Servs.*****, 865 S.W.2d 247, 253 (Tex. App. 1993). Even if the plaintiff consented to some conduct, the defendant can still be liable for acting outside the scope of the plaintiff's consent.** ***Oberman v. Gateway, Inc.*****, 853 S.W.2d 160, 172–73 (Tex. App. 1996).**

The rules and subrules were out of order; they should be written from broad to narrow, starting with the elements

A key subrule was missing; the facts of our case and the case illustration concern scope of consent, but the rule and explanation paragraph does not mention scope

The introductory sentence failed to show the key purpose for illustrating the case; it now shows the outcome and why it's important

Manipulating another's data more than that person consented to can constitute an invasion of privacy because consent is a matter of degree. ~~Exceeding the scope of a person's consent can constitute an invasion of privacy.~~ ***See id.*** **at 172–73. In** ***Oberman*****, the plaintiffs sued an app developer after learning the developer had uploaded all the data from their contacts files.** ***Id.*** **at 168.** ~~Yelp developed a Friend Finder feature that allowed Yelp users to locate other Yelp users by comparing email addresses of registered Yelp users to email addresses in the user's contact app. *Id.* at 168. This feature was available only to registered Yelp users, who had to agree to Yelp's terms of service and privacy policy. Yelp users brought a class action lawsuit against Yelp after they found out that Yelp had uploaded all of their contacts.~~ They argued they had agreed to let ~~Yelp~~ **the developer** access their contacts but not to upload them. ***Id.*** ~~That is similar to our case because Mr. Calhoon says he only authorized Mr. Potter to call an Uber, not to send a Tweet. Yelp moved for summary judgment,~~

Every sentence in a case illustration should cite to the case being illustrated

Too many factual details are included

Do not include facts about your case in the case illustration

Avoid procedural details of the illustrated case when possible

continued

~~which the court denied. *Id. at 173*~~. The court stated that "consent is only effective if the person alleging harm consented to the particular conduct or to substantially the same conduct and if the alleged tortfeasor did not exceed the scope of that consent" because "consent is not absolute, but rather a matter of degree." *Id.* at 172–73, 176. Based on the language of ~~Yelp's policies and procedures~~ **the plaintiffs' consent**, the court ~~concludes~~ **concluded** there ~~is~~ **was** a fact issue as to whether ~~Yelp~~ **the developer** acted within the scope of the users' consent or exceeded it by uploading their contacts rather than only accessing them. *Id.* at 173.

Case illustrations should be written in past tense

This is the sample answer without annotations:

> Invasion of privacy based on intrusion on seclusion has two elements: (1) an intentional intrusion on another's solitude, seclusion, or private affairs or concerns, which (2) would be highly offensive to a reasonable person. *Valenzuela v. Aquino*, 853 S.W.2d 512, 513 (Tex. 1993). When assessing whether an invasion is offensive, courts require the intrusion to be "unjustified or unwarranted." *Vaughn v. Drennon*, 202 S.W.3d 308, 320 (Tex. App. 2006). There can be no intrusion on seclusion if the plaintiff consented to the defendant's conduct. *Farrington v. Sysco Food Servs.*, 865 S.W.2d 247, 253 (Tex. App. 1993). Even if the plaintiff consented to some conduct, the defendant can still be liable for acting outside the scope of the plaintiff's consent. *Oberman v. Gateway, Inc.*, 853 S.W.2d 160, 172–73 (Tex. App. 1996).
>
> Manipulating another's data more than that person consented to can constitute an invasion of privacy because consent is a matter of degree. *See id.* In *Oberman*, the plaintiffs sued an app developer after learning the developer had uploaded all the data from their contacts files. *Id.* at 168. They argued they had agreed to let the developer access their contacts but not to upload them. *Id.* The court stated that "consent is only effective if the person alleging harm consented to the particular conduct or to substantially the same conduct and if the alleged tortfeasor did not exceed the scope of that consent" because "consent is not absolute, but rather a matter of degree." *Id.* at 172–73, 176. Based on the language of the plaintiffs' consent, the court concluded there was a fact issue as to whether the developer acted within the scope of the users' consent or exceeded it by uploading their contacts rather than only accessing them. *Id.* at 173.

Answer to Exercise 34

This chart shows which differences are legally significant and why:

FACT	DIFFERENCE LEGALLY SIGNIFICANT?	WHY OR WHY NOT?
Plaintiff's case: hunting in the woods Precedent case: hunting in a field	No	The location of the accident is irrelevant to whether the trigger mechanism was defectively designed.
Plaintiff's case: small amount of soft dirt found in trigger mechanism Precedent case: small amount of soft grass found in trigger mechanism	No	The plaintiff's case theory is that debris should not cause the rifle to malfunction. Grass and dirt are similar types of debris for this purpose.
Plaintiff's case: gun was a rifle Precedent case: gun was a pistol	Yes	The plaintiff's theory is specific to the particular type of gun involved in the accident, so what happened with another type of gun is irrelevant.
Plaintiff's case: gun owner shot a friend Precedent case: gun owner shot himself	No	Who was shot is irrelevant to whether the trigger mechanism was defectively designed.
Plaintiff's case: hunting in the day Precedent case: hunting at night	No	The time of day is irrelevant to whether the trigger mechanism was defectively designed.
Plaintiff's case: gun fired because debris prevented safety from working properly Precedent case: gun fired because safety was not turned on	Yes	The plaintiff's theory depends on debris interfering with the safety mechanism. An accidental discharge because the safety was never engaged is a completely different method of accidental discharge.

table continued

FACT	DIFFERENCE LEGALLY SIGNIFICANT?	WHY OR WHY NOT?
<u>Plaintiff's case</u>: rifle had a Baker trigger mechanism <u>Precedent case</u>: rifle had a different trigger mechanism (not Baker)	Yes	The plaintiff's theory is specific to a problem with the Baker trigger mechanism, so the operation of another type of trigger mechanism is irrelevant.
<u>Plaintiff's case</u>: gun banged into a tree <u>Precedent case</u>: gun banged into a rock	No	The misfire happened after a significant jolt. There is no functional difference between banging into a tree and into a rock.

Answer to Exercise 36

The application section should be organized around the main arguments that make up the affirmative argument: a thesis statement that summarizes all of the arguments, followed by topic sentences for each argument. The best choices below are in bold.

I. *Thesis Statement*

    A. Here, Sam will probably not be strictly liable because he had no specific indication that Skipper would bite a person.

    B. Here, the case of *Black v. Vinson* is helpful in resolving this issue.

    C. Here, Sam will probably not be strictly liable.

Comment: Option A is the best choice. It includes both main points that make up the entire argument and provides a conclusion. Option B does not give a conclusion. Option C gives a conclusion but gives no reason why, so it is not as helpful as it could be.

II. *First Topic Sentence*

    A. Sam did not know that his dog was aggressive.

    B. Sam knew Skipper was a "bit difficult."

    C. Sam had no specific sign that Skipper would bite, but only the vague piece of information that Skipper was a "bit difficult."

Comment: Option A provides a conclusion but lacks specific facts. Option B provides a fact but lacks information on why it matters. Option C is the best choice because it correctly provides an overview of the argument to follow.

III. *Second Topic Sentence*

    A. Neither the fact that Skipper is a pit bull nor his aggressiveness toward other animals predicts aggressiveness toward humans.

    B. Neither a dog's breed nor its aggressiveness toward other animals indicates future dangerousness toward humans.

    C. In the *Slack* case, neither the dog's breed nor its aggressiveness toward other animals was considered a prediction of future dangerousness.

Comment: Option A is the best choice because it correctly provides an overview of the argument to follow. Option B provides useful information about the law, and Option C provides helpful information about *Slack*, but the topic sentence should be about our case, not the precedent case.

Answer to Exercise 38

The application is missing specific references to precedent, which would be helpful in a fact-intensive inquiry such as this one. The reader will only see the point of comparisons if the items to be compared are placed near each other and the comparison's import is explained. The author of the application below has asked for critique; some suggestions for improvement are set out below. Suggested additions are in bold.

Here, Glory participated in business and public life without reaching general or limited public figure status. Glory's local political and business activities are insufficient to make him a general purpose public figure. Glory was a school board member and a member of a business association concerning fountain-building and installation. He was well known but only in limited business circles. **Pickens, on the other hand, wrote several business articles, but even this fell far short of the notoriety required to be a general purpose public figure.** *Id.* Glory's name was far from a household name. **Glory is similar to Pickens, who was not a public figure either.** *See id.*

The author has made several useful observations about Glory, but the equivalent facts about Pickens are buried in the explanation; reprise some of those facts here for a complete application section

Even as to limited purpose public figure status, Glory's facts present a weak case. There is no evidence of Glory penning articles for national publications or seeking the spotlight, **as Pickens did.** *See id.* Glory did serve as a school board member, but even if that or his professional activities rendered him a limited purpose public figure, such status is only relevant if the particular issue that the person thrust himself into is the same one as in the lawsuit. *Id.* **Just as in *Pickens*, where the public reputation concerned a different issue from the defamatory statements,** *see id.*, **the same is true here.** The lawsuit here is based on a stolen statue, while any limited purpose public figure status would be related to the fountain industry or the school board. This is an even weaker case than that of Pickens, who gave interviews and wrote articles for national business publications **yet was still not a public figure with regard to statements on an unrelated topic.** *See id.* **Thus, the allegedly defamatory statements are not protected by any limited purpose public figure status that Glory may have had.**

Legal principles in the application should contain citations to authority

Show the reader exactly how the present case compares to the precedent case by placing the information from each one side by side

Glory is therefore not a public figure for purposes of this lawsuit.

Remind the reader how current facts compare to facts in the precedent case

When comparing the outcome of our case to the precedent case, remind the reader how the precedent case turned out

This sentence explicitly states the inference from the preceding comparison

Answer to Exercise 40

This chart shows which application sentences are appropriate and explains why:

APPLICATION	APPROPRIATE?	WHY OR WHY NOT?
(1) Mr. Owens had notice that his dog was dangerous because his dog chewed through a fence last year.	No	No rule supports this analysis. The subrule provided only discusses prior bites. To make an effective argument based on chewing through a fence, either more rules are needed, or the analysis must be more in depth.
(2) Mr. Owens knew his dog was dangerous because his dog bit a child at the dog park in May.	Yes	This analysis applies a rule to clearly on-point facts.
(3) Mr. Owens had to know his dog was dangerous because it bit Ms. Cline five times and only a vicious dog would do that.	No	The tone is not objective. The analysis does not tie back to a rule or subrule.
(4) Mr. Owens knew his pit bull was inherently dangerous.	No	This statement is conclusory. Moreover, the rule stated that certain breeds could be considered inherently dangerous but did not provide examples. To make an effective argument based on inherent dangerousness, the writer needs either a case where a court has held that a pit bull is inherently dangerous or more case facts and analysis showing that pit bulls are inherently dangerous.

table continued

APPLICATION	APPROPRIATE?	WHY OR WHY NOT?
(5) Mr. Owens took reasonable measures to protect Ms. Cline from his dog by locking the dog in another room; the dog bit Ms. Cline only after she insisted on opening the door to the room.	Yes	This analysis applies a rule to clearly on-point facts.
(6) Mr. Owens kept his dog behind a locked fence and posted a "Beware of Dog" sign, just like the defendant in *Forest*.	No	This analysis refers to facts from *Forest* that were not included in the rules paragraph and is attempting to make an analogy-based argument. More information about *Forest* is necessary to make this argument.

Answer to Exercise 42

Here are sample applications for the two scenarios in the exercise:

Scenario 1

Comment: This scenario calls for a straightforward application of the rule because the client's facts fit well with the rule's guidelines. Analogical reasoning is unnecessary because the rule itself provides the answer.

Rick Bowman was detained because he was completely deprived of his liberty. The Georgia Code defines false imprisonment as an unlawful detention of another, where the person is "deprived of his personal liberty" for any length of time. Ga. Code Ann. § 51-7-20. Bowman was handcuffed to a chair, so he was completely unable to move. A person who is unable to move is deprived of his liberty, so he was detained.

Scenario 2

Comment: This scenario is not as straightforward as the first one, so analogies to the facts and reasoning of the precedent case are helpful here.

Here, Walker was probably detained because he remained at the store under the threat of arrest. The threat of arrest acted upon Walker's mind and intimidated him, just as the implied threat of violence intimidated the woman in *Smith. Smith v. Wal-Mart Stores E., LP*, 765 S.E.2d 518, 522 (Ga. Ct. App. 2014). Although there was no threat of physical violence in Walker's case, the threat need not be physical to cause a detention. *Id.* The *Smith* court made clear that a threat of "personal difficulty" could lead to a detention just as much as a threat of physical violence. *Id.* The manager's actions caused Walker to stay against his will and thus deprived Walker of his liberty. Walker was therefore probably detained.

Answer to Exercise 44

This chart shows which sentences should be used, sets out the correct order, and explains the choices:

SENTENCE	INCLUDE?	EXPLANATION AND ANY MODIFICATIONS
(5) Like the defendant's sister in *Lambert*, Ms. McDonald assisted in the abduction by giving her daughter money and provisions for the baby, knowing her daughter intended to abduct the baby.	Yes	This is a good thesis sentence. It sets up the coming analysis and is specific to the law and facts. No changes needed.
(3) Ms. McDonald gave her daughter money and supplies, which parallels Mr. Lambert's sister providing him with money and supplies.	Yes, with changes	Comparing the particular type of assistance given in both cases is important, but this sentence is not specific enough, and it is missing a citation. It should be rewritten to include more specific facts and a citation.
(1) Based on her daughter's statement about not being able to live only seeing the baby on weekends and the financial and material support she provided thereafter, a jury could infer that Ms. McDonald knew her daughter intended to abduct the baby, just as Mr. Lambert's sister knew of his intention and took out a loan a week in advance to have travel money to give him. *Id.*	Yes	This sentence provides specific facts and comparisons between the client's case and the precedent case and includes a citation. All precedent facts are included in the case illustration. No changes needed.
(7) And both the defendant here and in *Lambert* impeded the other parent's ability to locate the child by refusing to communicate. *Id.*	Yes, with changes	Comparing the refusal to communicate is important, and including more specifics about the communication would enhance the comparison.
(4) Thus, based on Ms. Simmons's statements to Ms. McDonald and the money and supplies she gave her daughter, Ms. McDonald likely assisted in the abduction.	Yes	The word "assisted" ties the conclusion back to the rule.

(2) Mr. Lambert's sister took out a loan in advance, gave him the money, gave him clothes for the child, took him to the airport, and refused to call back the child's mother, just as Ms. McDonald knew her daughter was distraught over the custody arrangements, gave her money, gave her diapers and formula, and would not return the mother's calls or texts.	No	This sentence contains far too many facts to make a helpful comparison. The client facts and precedent case facts should be woven together, not merely recited in full, side by side.
(6) Mr. Lambert's sister took him to the airport, but Ms. McDonald did not take her daughter anywhere.	No	This comparison is factually correct but irrelevant to the analysis and should thus be excluded.
(8) The defendant was liable in *Lambert* when she helped an abductor, so Ms. McDonald should be liable too.	No	This sentence is too generic to be helpful, either as a thesis sentence or in the analysis.

This is the sample answer, with all sentences that should be included (as modified) in the correct order:

> Like the defendant's sister in *Lambert*, Ms. McDonald assisted in the abduction by giving her daughter money and provisions for the baby, knowing her daughter intended to abduct the baby. Ms. McDonald gave her daughter money, along with food and diapers, which parallels Mr. Lambert's sister providing him with money, clothing for the child, and transportation to the airport. *Id.* Based on her daughter's statement about not being able to live only seeing the baby on weekends and the financial and material support she provided thereafter, a jury could infer that Ms. McDonald knew her daughter intended to abduct the baby, just as Mr. Lambert's sister knew of his plans and took out a loan a week in advance to have travel money to give him. *Id.* And, both the defendant here and in *Lambert* impeded the other parent's ability to locate the child by refusing to either talk to or text with the parent. *Id.* Thus, based on Ms. Simmons's statements to Ms. McDonald and the money and supplies she gave her daughter, Ms. McDonald likely assisted in the abduction.

Answer to Exercise 46

This chart shows which sentences should be used for the counterargument and rebuttal, their correct order, and the reasons for these choices:

SENTENCE	INCLUDE?	EXPLANATION
(5) Coulson will argue that he contemporaneously experienced with his sense of hearing an unusual sound and within seconds saw Leo unconscious on the pavement after being hit by a car.	Yes	The transition into counterargument is obvious, thereby minimizing the risk of reader confusion, and the statement of the counterargument is clear.
(8) He will likely emphasize that although he did not see the accident, sensorial perception by its very terms includes senses other than vision; that another sense, here his hearing, took a few seconds to process the incident does not make his perception of the accident any less contemporaneous.	Yes	Counterarguments—particularly strong ones, as in this case—should be explained in detail.
(1) Even so, a court will probably reject this argument.	Yes	This sentence signals the transition from counterargument to rebuttal, with an appropriate level of certainty to reflect the strength of the counterargument.
(6) Because a bystander claim is an exception to the general rule against negligent infliction of emotional distress claims, a court will probably construe it narrowly to avoid the exception swallowing the rule.	Yes	The reasoning behind the rule can often be used to fortify a rebuttal.
(4) Coulson did not know that the thump he heard was anything troubling until he heard the driver's exclamation, and by that point, the accident was over.	Yes	The rebuttal emphasizes the specific facts to highlight the gap between Coulson's sensory input and his knowledge of the accident.

(3) Thus, because Coulson observed only the aftermath of the accident and not the accident itself, he probably cannot meet the second condition for bystander recovery.	Yes	A strong conclusion justifies the initial prediction and ensures the reader understands the rebuttal is concluded.
(7) This argument will fail.	No	This transition from the counterargument to rebuttal is too forcefully worded. The counterargument is strong, and this is a close call. An overly confident rebuttal would be misleading.
(2) Coulson did not see the accident, and so he cannot recover as a bystander as a matter of law, no matter what he saw after the accident.	No	This misstates the law. The law speaks to sensory perception, and that includes senses other than sight.

This is how the counterargument and rebuttal would look with all the proper sentences in the correct order:

> Coulson will argue that he contemporaneously experienced with his sense of hearing an unusual sound and within seconds saw Leo unconscious on the pavement after being hit by a car. He will likely emphasize that although he did not see the accident, sensorial perception by its very terms includes senses other than vision; that another sense, here his hearing, took a few seconds to process the incident does not make his perception of the accident any less contemporaneous. Even so, a court will probably reject this argument. Because a bystander claim is an exception to the general rule against negligent infliction of emotional distress claims, a court will probably construe it narrowly to avoid the exception swallowing the rule. Coulson did not know that the thump he heard was anything troubling until he heard the driver's exclamation, and by that point, the accident was over. Thus, because Coulson observed only the aftermath of the accident and not the accident itself, he probably cannot meet the second condition for bystander recovery.

Answer to Exercise 48

Here are five specific problems with counterargument and rebuttal in the exercise. The comment boxes below the table provide additional explanation:

1. The first sentence does not clearly signal the beginning of a counterargument and will confuse the reader.

2. The counterargument is not explained in any detail and refers generally to a legal standard without citation.

3. The counterargument does not include language acknowledging its function as a counterargument, meaning the reader might be confused because the sentence appears to contradict the prior analysis.

4. The rebuttal is too vague and does not specifically rebut the counterargument or provide any new analysis.

5. The final conclusion to the argument is missing, thus leaving the reader to speculate as to how you reached your ultimate prediction.

The reader will likely not recognize this as the beginning of a counterargument

The reader will likely be confused by the seeming contradiction

The other entries on the spreadsheet are relevant. They are all about error code 55, and that is close enough since the other incidents do not need to be identical. But a court would probably disagree with this because they are not identical.

This language is vague

What case is this from? Authority must be included

This is an improved counterargument and rebuttal paragraph that clearly transitions to and explains the counterargument, with authority, followed by an explicit rebuttal and ultimate conclusion that justifies your prediction:

The counterargument's beginning is clearly signaled

The counterargument is explained in detail, with language clearly showing that it is a counterargument

This strong conclusion justifies the prediction

> Ms. Mulder will likely argue that all prior error code 55 warranty claims are admissible because the standard specifies that the prior incidents need only be sufficiently similar but "not necessarily identical." *ABC Motors*, 422 S.W.3d at 905. According to this theory, the high number of airbag code 55 claims—78 in only two years—on the exact make and model of her car would show Wesla had notice of a problem with its airbag design, and if it had acted appropriately, she may never have been injured. This argument is unlikely to prevail. Though Ms. Mulder is correct that the prior incidents need not be identical, they must be similar enough to be relevant. *See id*. Merely having the same error code does not establish sufficient similarity when that error code is undisputedly generated by two independent types of connector malfunctions, only one of which is at issue in this case. Ms. Mulder cannot meet her burden of proving that Wesla knew of a defect for connector A based on a different connector (connector B) failing a certain number of times or other error code 55 incidents based on a reason not recorded in the spreadsheet. Therefore, a court is likely to admit only the portion of the spreadsheet involving claims specifically related to connector A claims.

The relevant rule is quoted and cited

A clear transition from counterargument to rebuttal is provided

The rebuttal is fully explained and explicitly addresses the counterargument with additional reasons

Answer to Exercise 50

This chart shows which sentences should be included in the conclusion and explains why:

SENTENCES	INCLUDE?	EXPLANATION
(2) Beety's claim against Big K will likely fail on both the breach of duty and causation elements. Because Big K cleaned the floor regularly and the coffee spill she slipped on had been on the floor for only one minute, Big K likely did not breach any duty. Further, Beety injured her back in a car accident a month before she slipped in the store, so the car accident, not the slip, likely caused her damages.	Yes	The conclusion is immediate and clear, followed by the essential reasoning on each element. The prediction language matches the introduction.
(5) We may also have a good argument that Big K owed Beety no duty as a matter of law because the condition that caused her fall—a spilled cup of coffee brought in from outside the store—was not within Big K's control. If you would like me to research and analyze this issue, please let me know.	Yes	It is appropriate to provide advice or other ideas for potential arguments or research in a memo, but only in the conclusion section, as done here.
(1) Beety's claim against Big K will fail.	No	No explanation is given for the conclusion, and the strength of the prediction is stronger than provided in the introduction.

(3) Liability flows from conduct that causes reasonably foreseeable harm. *Bossley v. Smith*, 555 S.W.3d 290, 295 (Tex. 2018). A harm is foreseeable if a person of ordinary intelligence should have reasonably anticipated the danger. *Id.*	No	The conclusion typically does not need rules and subrules and should be short and to the point. Further, citations are not needed in the conclusion.
(4) Big K also probably owed Beety no duty as a matter of law because the condition that caused her fall—a spilled cup of coffee brought in from outside the store—was not within Big K's control.	No	Though this conclusion provides the basic reason supporting it, the sentence is inappropriate because it contains a new conclusion not stated in the introduction or otherwise in the memo.

This is how the two sentences come together to form a memo conclusion:

> Beety's claim against Big K will likely fail on both the breach of duty and causation elements. Because Big K cleaned the floor regularly and the coffee spill she slipped on had been on the floor for only one minute, Big K likely did not breach any duty. Further, Beety injured her back in a car accident a month before she slipped in the store, so the car accident, not the slip, likely caused her damages. We may also have a good argument that Big K owed Beety no duty as a matter of law because the condition that caused her fall—a spilled cup of coffee brought in from outside the store—was not within Big K's control. If you would like me to research and analyze this issue, please let me know.

Answer to Exercise 52

Although the content of the email excerpt is good, the formatting makes the content difficult to read, particularly on a phone or tablet screen. Breaking the material up into paragraphs with white space in between, adding headings, and explicitly enumerating items will substantially improve the email. This is how the same excerpt looks with those adjustments:

Ms. Maddux,

You asked me to analyze whether our client, Mr. Burger, could be vicariously liable for the conduct of its employee in assaulting a customer. Mr. Burger would likely not be vicariously liable because the employee was acting outside the course and scope of his employment when he angrily assaulted a customer.

<u>Facts.</u> Johnny Hudson worked for Mr. Burger, taking orders and serving food. Austin Parks, a Mr. Burger customer, became upset when he did not have his food ten minutes after placing his order. Parks started berating Hudson, who was working behind the counter and had taken Parks's order. Hudson responded by throwing a milkshake blender at Parks, hitting him in the head. Parks has sued Hudson and Mr. Burger, asserting Mr. Burger is vicariously liable for Parks's assault.

<u>Analysis.</u> Employers can be vicariously liable for a worker's tort if the worker is

    (1) an employee,

    (2) acting in the course and scope of employment,

    (3) at the time of the tortious conduct.

Wisenhouse v. Armendez, 14 S.W.3d 200, 201 (Tex. App. 2000).

Hudson was on shift working for Mr. Burger when he threw the milkshake blender at Parks, and thus the timing element is not an issue. This memo will address whether Hudson was an employee at the time of the assault and, if so, whether he was acting in the course and scope of his employment when he assaulted Parks.

(1) **Employee.** Hudson was likely a Mr. Burger employee because Mr. Burger controlled all essential details of Hudson's work. [Additional analysis would be included here.]

(2) **Course and Scope.** Because Hudson acted out of anger and not to further Mr. Burger's business, however, Hudson was probably not acting in the course and scope of his employment, and thus Mr. Burger will probably not be vicariously liable for his conduct. [Additional analysis would be included here.]

Answer to Exercise 54

This is a sample of how the single-issue memo in Chapter 8 could be written as an email memo:

> Subject: Reasonableness of Elaine Swift's request to bring outside food to Fun Zone
>
> Ms. Maldonado,
>
> Our client, Elaine Swift, has severe food allergies. You asked me to evaluate the reasonableness under the Americans with Disabilities Act of her request that Fun Zone modify its policy against outside food so she could safely have her birthday party there. Her request was likely reasonable because she didn't demand that Fun Zone prepare safe food, and sharing food with her guests is an important part of the party experience.
>
> <u>Facts.</u> Elaine's potentially fatal food allergies prevent her from safely eating any food at Fun Zone. Fun Zone requires mandatory food and drink purchases for all parties and prohibits outside food. Elaine asked to bring all the food for her and her party guests so that she could have the same party experience as any other child by sharing a safe birthday cake and other food with them. Fun Zone refused, saying it would only allow Elaine to bring in food for herself.
>
> <u>Analysis.</u> Because Elaine's request to supply her own food didn't require Fun Zone to take any affirmative actions and would have allowed her to enjoy a typical party experience, the request was likely reasonable. A place of public accommodation such as Fun Zone can be liable under the ADA for failing "to make reasonable modifications" to policies to accommodate a disability unless those modifications would "fundamentally alter the nature of the business." 42 U.S.C. § 12182(a), (b)(2)(A)(ii). It is undisputed that Fun Zone is a covered entity and that Elaine's food allergies are a disability, and (as will be explained below) fundamental alteration is an unpleaded affirmative defense, so the only issue is whether Elaine's modification request was reasonable.
>
> • **Reasonableness.** The plaintiff must prove that a modification request is reasonable, which means that it is reasonable generally or "in the run of cases." This inquiry varies case by case, focusing on factors such as the nature of the disability and cost. *Johnson v. Gambrinus Co./ Spoetzl Brewery*, 116 F.3d 1052, 1058 (5th Cir. 1997); *Vorhees v. Pizza Place, Inc.*, 393 F. Supp. 3d 203, 212 (S.D. Tex. 2018).

continued

Elaine's request for Fun Zone to modify its outside food policy was likely reasonable. Elaine can't safely eat any of Fun Zone's food without risking a potentially fatal allergic reaction. An accommodation to allow her to enjoy a party at Fun Zone without risking death seems facially reasonable. Elaine would still pay for her party, Fun Zone wouldn't need to prepare safe food or otherwise take any actions to ensure her safety, and Elaine can enjoy a regular party experience with her friends.

Fun Zone has said it acted reasonably because it offered to allow Elaine to bring in food for herself. But enacting Fun Zone's proposal would deprive Elaine of the experience of sharing food, particularly a birthday treat like a cake. And even if Fun Zone's option were reasonable, that misses the point: the defendant counter-proposing a different reasonable option does not render the plaintiff's option unreasonable.

• **Fundamental Alteration.** The reasonableness of a requested modification is distinct from whether the modification would fundamentally alter the nature of the business. The reasonable modification inquiry focuses on "the general nature of the accommodation" while fundamental alteration, which is an affirmative defense, examines "the specifics of the plaintiff's or defendant's circumstances." *See Johnson*, 116 F.3d at 1059–60.

Fun Zone has not, at this point, pleaded fundamental alteration as an affirmative defense. Even so, it has claimed that forcing it to allow anyone with a food restriction to have a birthday party without the revenue from food sales would undermine its business model and be much too costly. That argument goes to the specifics of Fun Zone's circumstances rather than the overall general reasonableness of modifying an outside food ban to allow an allergic patron to supply her own food. That's a fundamental alteration argument, and since fundamental alteration is unpleaded at this point, it has no role in the litigation.

<u>Next Steps.</u> Given Fun Zone's pleading deficiency, I didn't evaluate the merits of a fundamental alteration defense. If you anticipate that Fun Zone might amend its pleadings to assert a fundamental alteration defense and would like for me to conduct further research and analysis on that issue or any other, please let me know.

Joe